Books by:

Carol Susan DeVaney-Wong

DeVaney-Wong International Workbook: A Resource for Trainers and Facilitators (2014)

Managing Diversity, ITC, distributed by HRD Press (1993) (workbook, manual, and video)

C. Eldon Taylor and Carol Susan DeVaney-Wong

Golden Dreams: Companion to Hellfires of Grief (2013)

Golden Dreams II: Companion to Hellfires of Grief II (2014)

C. Eldon Taylor

Hellfires of Grief: Love Poems (2013)

Hellfires of Grief II: More Love Poems (2014)

DeVaney-Wong International Workbook

A Resource for Trainers and Facilitators

Carol Susan DeVaney-Wong

DeVaney-Wong International Workbook
A Resource for Trainers and Facilitators

by Carol Susan DeVaney-Wong

©2014 C. Eldon Taylor

ISBN: 061599489X
ISBN-13: 978-0615994895

LCCN: 2014906523

Printed in USA
by CreateSpace
an Amazon.com Company

Published by
C. Eldon Taylor
Henrico, Virginia 23228
celdontaylor@gmail.com

to
trainers
and
facilitators

Introduction

The **DeVaney-Wong International Workbook** (**DeVaney-Wong Workbook**) is a collection of sixteen modules of handouts and converted power point presentations developed by Carol Susan DeVaney-Wong for use in training and facilitation. A master facilitator and organizational development expert, Carol Susan's materials provide a framework that may suggest valuable ideas for others. Topics include communication and conflict management, change and change management, diversity and inclusion, strategic planning, and management and leadership.

Inspiration

The inspiration for the **DeVaney-Wong Workbook** started in early December 2013 looking through boxes seeking other documents. I kept finding Carol Susan's training and facilitation materials. With each discovery I would think "a shame this material is not available to share with others who might find it of value." In February 2014 I dreamed I was compiling Carol Susan's materials into a workbook. The title was provided in the dream. Upon awakening I realized sharing Carol Susan's materials is inspired work.

Fair Use of *DeVaney-Wong Workbook*

The contents of the **DeVaney-Wong Workbook** are considered fair use materials meaning copying is not only permitted but encouraged. Exceptions include the DeVaney-Wong dragon logo, the gold dragon logo, and the work of others used with permission.

CD Availability

To facilitate sharing and use of the *DeVaney-Wong Workbook* materials a CD is available that includes the materials of the *DeVaney-Wong Workbook* plus a bonus of sixteen power point presentations (357 slides). Information about obtaining the *DeVaney-Wong Workbook CD* and list of bonus power point presentations can be found in the second appendix (pages 401-403). Information is also available at **www.devaneywong.org**.

Donations

For each copy of the *DeVaney-Wong Workbook* purchased a donation of one dollar ($1.00) will be made by the publisher to the Pancreatic Cancer Action Network (PanCan: www.pancan.org) to support PanCan's initiatives to educate providers, decision makers, and the general community.

It is my hope, wish, and intent that you find the *DeVaney-Wong Workbook* a helpful resource in your training and facilitation work.

C. Eldon Taylor

Publisher

March 2014

DeVaney-Wong International Workbook
A Resource for Trainers and Facilitators

Table of Contents

COMMUNICATION and CHANGE

DIVERSITY & INCLUSION

LEADERSHIP

APPENDIX 1: Remembering Carol Susan

APPENDIX 2: Other Information

COMMUNICATION
and
CHANGE

COMMUNICATION and CHANGE

Effective Communication
&
Conflict Management

September 15-16, 2009
Minneapolis (Bloomington), Minnesota

facilitated by

Carol Susan DeVaney, CPF, CPLP
DeVaney Wong International, LLC

For Your Notes..

Agenda

Morning

- Introductions

- Objectives and Participant Expectations

- Fundamentals of Communication

- Test Your Listening Skills

- Assess Your Listening Style

- Elements of an Effective Message – A Communication Model

(Lunch Break)

Afternoon

- Elements of —Culture‖ in Communication

- Preparing for Potentially Difficult Communication

- Persuasion

- The Conflict Radar

- Assessing Your Conflict Style

- Fundamentals for Positive Conflict Management

- Practice

- Closing and Evaluation

Objectives

Participants will...

✓ learn a model for effective communication

✓ evaluate their listening skills

✓ assess their listening styles

✓ improve their ability to engage in important communication

✓ discover their conflict style

✓ explore ways to prevent and resolve conflict

✓ practice realistic scenarios

Communication Model

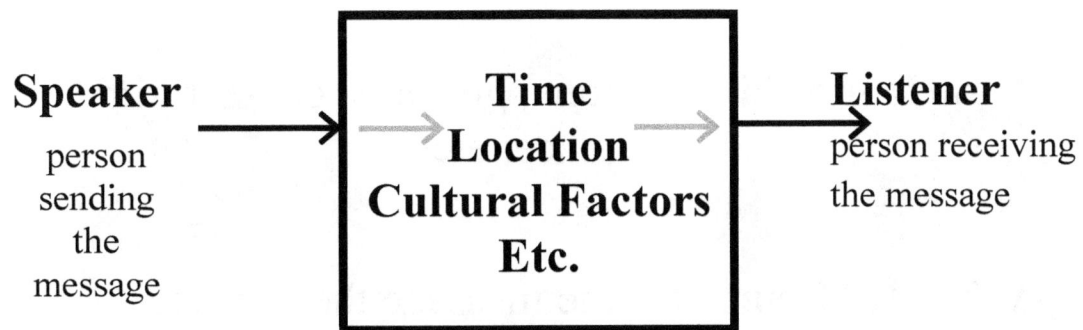

Speaker	**Time**	**Listener**
person sending the message	**Location** **Cultural Factors** **Etc.**	person receiving the message

Spoken words account for 30-35% of the meaning
of a message.

Three Parts of the Message

What Is Said = the actual words

How It Is Said = tone, gestures, context, time, place, etc.

What Is Meant = the message the speaker attempts to deliver

Listening Skills

High levels of —emotional intelligence‖ are correlated with good listening skills.

From a list of items, people can remember about 7.

With last words of unrelated sentences the average is 2.8 items.

People can recall about 17% of the content of the evening news. If prompted they can recall about 25%.

A person can talk at a rate of 125-175 words per minute. We can listen at up to 450 words per minute.

30-35% of how we understand a message is the spoken word.

In business and academic settings listening is in the top 3 skills noted for successful leaders.

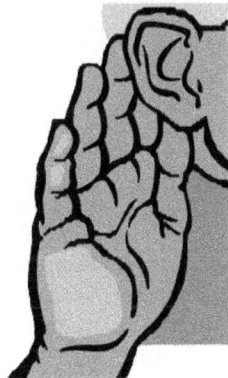

Listener Preference

P = **People**

A = **Action**

C = **Content**

T = **Time**

Listening Strategies

—**Affirmative listening** tries to silence our internal critic by trying to hear everything and seeking out new ideas, common ground, and shared beliefs and looking at it as an opportunity to learn more about the person and the situation.

Sometimes if you suspect there will be resistance to hearing what you have to say, you can acknowledge this out loud, like: —I know what I am going to say may sound unreasonable, but can you help me out by hearing it all the way through? This is called —Couching.

Questions To Ask Yourself

?   Was I listening affirmatively?

?   Did I clarify that I understand what you meant?

?   What am I supposed to do with this information?

Four Reasons People Communicate

To Persuade Someone

↑

To Provide Information

↑

To Express Their Feelings

↑

To Establish Contact

**Teaching People Skills
in "Crucial Confrontations"
has resulted in...**

- **40% ↑ in productivity**

- **30% ↑ in quality**

- **50% ↓ in costs**

- **20% ↑ in employee satisfaction**

—from Vital Smarts research

Conflict Styles

1) **Avoiding**

2) **Smoothing**

3) **Forcing**

4) **Bargaining**

5) **Problem Solving**

The Conflict Radar at Work

Sometimes we are so busy or distracted that we find ourselves surprised or blindsided into a conflict situation. The following are strategies that will help you identify potential conflict early to prevent and/or resolve it.

1)   **Think Ahead** — As you go about your daily business think about the Who, What, When, How, Why or Where of potential conflict.

2)   **Ask for Information** — Find out how others are feeling or what they are thinking about issues, situations or people. Don't assume you know.

3)   **Inform** — Let others know how you think or feel in open but non-threatening ways.

4)   **Future Focused** — Try to keep the conversation moving towards the future. In other words: What could be possible? What would success look like? What is the person's interest, not position?

Setting the Stage

Think Before You Speak!

?   Are you confronting about the right problem or issue?

?   Are you ready to discuss the issue with the other person as a person and not as the enemy?

How do you know if you have the right problem?

?   Do the solutions you get achieve the results you want?

?   Do you find yourself constantly going back to discuss the same problem?

?   Do you find yourself getting more worked up than the —problem‖ should be causing?

Three Levels of a Problem

Level I   The first time it happens you may just want to describe it.

Level II   The next time it happens you need to describe the fact that this may be a pattern of behavior.

Level III   If the problem continues to reoccur, you need to discuss how it affects the relationship.

And the Problem Is?

Your teenage daughter got her driver's license last week. She drives herself and her two best friends to her first big dance 20 minutes away. You have discussed your concerns and she agreed to come home by 11 p.m. and take her cell phone in case of an emergency. She is now an hour late, and when you try to call her cell phone, it rings in her bedroom where she left it. She comes in 1¼ hours late.

1) What is the problem?

2) Describe it in one sentence.

$$C = \text{Content}$$

$$P = \text{Pattern}$$

$$R = \text{Relationship}$$

from <u>Crucial Confrontations</u>

Problems typically are not the behavior, but the actual consequences of the behavior.

Other times the problem is not about the behavior or the consequences but about the person's original intentions.

So what is it that you want or don't want for you, the other person, and for the relationship?

Be careful: Silence may not make the problem go away.

Keep Focused on the Future

Basically conversations occur in...

Past   What got us here / History

Present What is happening or what is
about to happen

Future   What you would like to
imagine happening

Some Tips for Future Focus

1)   The **past** establishes a connection to the future, but it's historical, so it involves what worked or did not work then. It does not address the present or the future.

—We tried that before and it did not work.

2)   **Present** conversation involved what is currently happening or what is about to happen. It involves current action.

—When our meeting ends today, I will call and get some pricing.

3)   **Future**-focused conversation is a conversation that focuses on possibilities or potential.

—What if we could figure out a way to speed production without compromising safety?

The Request — A Tool of Persuasion

Usually people will only change what they are doing if they see what is in it for them: **pain** or **gain**.

A **request** is a change-focused conversation. It has three parts:

1) **What** do you want done

2) **When** does it need to be done

3) **Who** is going to do it

New Order:

PAST → FUTURE → PRESENT

Unfair Communication Techniques

1) **Pretending that the other person has made an unreasonable statement or demand.**

   —You make such a big deal out of nothing!

2) **Jumping to conclusions or "mind reading."**

   —Don't even try. I know what you want.

3) **Switching the subject.**

   —That reminds me, do you remember what we talked about last week...?

4) **Bringing up more than one accusation at a time.**

   —Not only are you inconsiderate but you're lazy too!

5) **Bragging or keeping score.**

   —You don't try as hard as I do.

6) **Being logical when someone is talking about their feelings.**

   —Don't be so dramatic. You'll get another job.

7) **Interrupting.**

   —Excuse me but. . . .

8) **Intimidating, yelling, or exploding.**

   —You *(censored)* of a *(censored)*!

9) **Denying the other person's experience.**

   —You shouldn't feel like that.

10) **Using <u>You</u> rather that <u>I</u> statements.**

   —You really make me angry!

Translation

Directions: In your small group try to translate the following statement into the language you have been assigned.

"I need you to stop touching that piece of equipment when you are not wearing gloves."

Translation . . .

Over My Head

You have had three Non-Critical, Pre-Operative Sanitation issues in the past month. All three times the production manager, Bill, has had an excuse why these issues were not corrected. You decide to notify your immediate supervisor regarding this situation.

Bill, the production manager finds out that you spoke to your supervisor, and confronts you. He says this was something the two of you could have fixed without bringing in your supervisor. He hints that you have had it out for him since you began working here, three months ago.

How would you respond? Is this conversation in the past, present, or future?

Our Jobs Depend on You

You are one of two graders working at a facility in a rural town. Basically, the processing plant offers one of the few employment opportunities around.

In the past, you and Sally, the other grader, have had a very good working relationship with plant management. Recently, some equipment has malfunctioned, damaging products and holding up production.

Plant management set up a —temporary shortcut‖ to keep production flowing. You feel their solution raises several quality concerns. Sally shares the same concerns as you, but is fearful that pushing the issue would stop production.
Considering the plant is facing serious financial issues due to the high cost of grain and fuel does not help ease Sally's fears.

Both, Sally's son and the production manager's son play softball with your son. At a recent game, the production supervisor asks you if you can do him a favor. —Can you please hold off addressing the quality issues until we get our equipment fixed?
After all, if you force us to buy expensive equipment that we have no budget for, we could all lose our jobs, including you and Sally.‖

How would you handle this?

None of Your Business

You come in around noon from a doctor's appointment and see two employees in the parking lot that seemed to be smoking what you think is marijuana. When they see you, they quickly put what they were smoking out and move the car to another part of the lot.

You have noticed that these two workers have seemed rather distracted several times while on the line this last month, but as far as you know they have not had any special safety concerns or absenteeism problems.

Is this any of your business? If yes, what would you do?

What Did You Say?

The plant you work at has always had a relaxed, fun environment where folks go to happy hour after work and joke freely with each other.

Recently two supervisors have been hired that are supposedly from a very conservative religion that you don't know much about.

You were teasing one of the other supervisors about what he was going to do for Christmas. Both of you asked the newcomers about Santa and whether they were going to have a tree.

For some reason the new people felt this was too personal and were offended that somehow you were making fun of their faith.

Honestly, you have no idea what you said that was offensive. You have to work closely with these folks and it has caused a lot of tension on the team.

What can you do?

Not Now!

You are one of three graders at a large plant. You come in for your shift and see one of the other graders, Ted, scolding the plant manager for the —dock needing a good sweep.

This seems like incredibly bad timing, as the manager is literally under a machine fixing a major problem. You and Ted get along fine at this plant, but several people have expressed irritation with Ted's impatience, apparent lack of concern for anything else that the person is involved in, and —nitpicking.

To be honest, they are probably right. Ted is a by-the-book guy who, if in doubt, goes with the most conservative interpretation of everything. You don't know what is going on with him personally, but he never seems to be in a good mood.

You are not Ted's supervisor. What, if anything, can you do?

Suggested Readings

The Emotional Intelligence Quick Book. Travis Bradberry and Jean Greaves. Simon & Schuster, 2005.

Multicultural Manners. Norine Dresser. John Wiley, 1996.

Crucial Conversations. Kerry Patterson, Joseph Grenny, Ron McMillan and Al Switzer. McGraw Hill, 2002.

Crucial Confrontations. Kerry Patterson, Joseph Grenny, Ron McMillan and Al Switzer. McGraw Hill, 2005.

The Power of Appreciative Inquiry. Diana Whitney and Amanda Trosten-Bloom. Berrett-Koehler, 2003.

For Your Notes..

Managing Change

Practical Knowledge and Skills
In Today's Changing Workplace

Ft. Lauderdale, Florida
October 2008

Presented by

Carol-Susan DeVaney, CPF, CPLP
DeVaney-Wong International, LLC

For Your Notes

Agenda

- Pretest – Introductions

- Why Do People and Organizations Change?

- Individual Reactions to Change

- Phases in Organizational Change

- Forces Pushing for Change in Government

- What We Know Works in Effective Change

- What Can You Do?

- Common Situation – A Time for Practice

- What Next?

- Closing and Evaluation

Objectives

- Learn about individual and organizational reactions to change

- Understand the forces that push change

- Gain insight into what works and what doesn't work when it comes to change

- Practice how to deal with common scenarios that can occur during a time of change.

- Have Fun!

Two Questions

1) What helps me manage change effectively?

2) When have I been successful at a change and what made it work?

Pain or Gain

There are only two reasons why organizations or individuals undergo a change process.

  Current or Anticipated PAIN

  Current or Anticipated GAIN

Pain is generated because of problems or because opportunities are missed.

Common Reactions Individuals Have To Change

1)   People will feel awkward, ill at ease and self-conscious.

2)   People will be concerned about what they have to give up –
      loss.

3)   People will be concerned that they don't have enough time,
      money, know-how or other resources.

4)   People can handle only so much change at a time.

5)   People are ready for and react to change differently.

6)   People will feel alone even if everyone else is going through
      the change.

7)   There is the tendency to want things to go back to how they
      were.

Phases or Stages of Organizational Change

1) Denial/Disbelief

People act as if nothing is happening. There is a general numbness.
There is apathy and a sense of "this too will pass."
Disbelief that "they really mean" the change.
Focus is on the past and you see lots of activity but little end result.

The most important task for the manager is to confront the individuals with truthful information. Let them know the change will happen, what is expected from them and how they can prepare themselves.

Worst thing to do: Bring in a motivational speaker or celebrate.

2) Resistance/Grief

Here you see anger, disappointment and opposition. Groups round up the wagons; lack of cooperation. There is a sense of generalized negativity. Here you may see accidents, absenteeism, illnesses, and general acting out.

The most important task for the manager is to allow the feelings to emerge and to manage the conflict.

Worst thing to do: Not allow people the opportunity to express apprehensions, fears, concerns.

3) **Trial & Error**

People begin to try new things. As a manager this can be an overwhelming time because people deluge you with new ideas and suggestions. The group feels like there is too much to do and not a clear focus or direction. You see people slowly beginning to accept the change but many are anxious about the new skills they must learn. The task for the manager here is to help set goals, help prioritize and help facilitate problem solving.

Worst thing to do: We are never experts at something new. Reward steps in the right direction. Don't wait for complete success to reward.

4) **Acceptance/Involvement**

People begin to see the change as "the way it is." They begin to actively participate and contribute to the change. You see people initiating their work again and individuals begin to become teams again.

The task of the manager is to facilitate "team building."

Worst thing to do: Do not be surprised when people slide back. It is important that you keep consistently focused on where you want to go.

**Don't Let Change
Knock You Off Your Feet**

Tip Sheet for Coping with Change

1)   Give yourself permission to be in a learning posture. We all need time to understand and adjust to change.

2)   Keep a check on your anticipatory anxiety. Often the anticipation of the unknown is more stressful than the actual event.

3)   Sort out what you can and can't control. Try to keep yourself in a position where you can make some of the choices even if they are small ones.

4)   Get help. Others may not realize you need help, or they may not know what kind of help you need.

5)   Don't compare yourself to others who are going through similar situations. They can be a great source of support, but everyone does not react the same to risk and ambiguity.

6)   Take time out to recharge. Sometimes we get so involved in the change process we lose total perspective on the situation.

7)   It is a struggle to leave the old behind, but in doing so, we face new experiences and opportunities.

8)   Give yourself credit. You did not get to the age you are without having some success at managing change. Review those successes and make them work for you.

Breaking Old Assumptions

Loyalty & Security

Traditional <u>LOYALTY</u> assumes a reciprocal dependent relationship. I, the worker, am loyal to you and you in turn will take care of me = <u>SECURITY</u>.

Organizations cannot offer security because security is totally dependent on the customer. As long as the customer sees your product as valuable, you get to keep your job.

Seniority & Continuous Learning

The assumption that seniority gave us a special edge is being challenged since skills are becoming obsolete in much shorter increments.

The worker who is keeping up not only with current but also with emerging technologies is now prized. This worker may not have as much "experience" or age.

Incremental vs. Constant Change

Customer demands, global competition and constantly changing technology do not always allow the luxury of incremental change.

Those who can see constant turmoil as the way business will be done, and not as a temporary phenomenon, will survive.

Phases in an Organization's Development

Start Up Few people, long hours. Rules being made up as needed. Salaries usually not good. Lots of unknowns but room for creativity.

Acceleration Rapid growth and customer demands. Loose structure and people take on multiple roles. Much uncertainty. Thin line between success and chaos. Constant need for more/different resources.

Organization Growth begins to stabilize and formal structure gets put in place to manage it. Employees begin to have some longevity and the organization has a clear sense of history.

Maturation Distinct established culture. Lots of structure and procedures. Implementing change more difficult because boundaries more rigid. What has made them successful in the past can hurt their future.

Levels of Change

Cosmetic   This is when you make minor, incremental, cosmetic or simply accommodating changes.

Structural   This is when change involves the whole organization. It involves developing new ways of operating.

Transformational   Most radical of all change. It is breaking the paradigm. It is sudden and extensive. It redefines what you do and who you are as an organization.

<u>Note</u>: Reengineering is transformational change with the assistance of emerging technologies.

The level of change is dependent on two major factors.

- Is the change reactive or proactive?

- To be a success, will all or only parts of the organization be involved?

Assessing Your Strengths/Vulnerability

1)   How has the current organizational climate impacted you and your organization?

2)   What are you currently doing to keep ahead of new technologies and expectations?

3)   Who are your mentors? Are they the appropriate choices?

4)   What shape is your network in?

5)   What helps you cope with constant change?

Paradigms

1)   What are some of the negative paradigms that exist in your organization?

2)   What are some paradigms that negatively affect my department? my team?

3)   What are some paradigms I am operating under that may not be effective?

4)   What can I do to challenge assumptions?

From Entitlement To Performance

ENTITLEMENT

Low Levels

People are flexible, innovative, have confidence in each other and hold each other accountable.

High Levels

People avoid taking risks, are dependent and focus on rules and rule checking. Very little accountability.

Atmosphere

Avoiding risk is more important than accomplishment.

FEAR

Low Levels

High respect for leadership and peers. Sense of security and control over one's work. High morale and teamwork.

High Levels

Cynicism and feelings of vulnerability abound. Lots of stress and empire building. The denial of any problems is common.

Atmosphere

Everything seems chaotic. People are focused on saving themselves.

PERFORMANCE

Low Levels

Lots of dependence and focus on how it was done before. Everyone seeking to protect themselves and their turf.

High Levels

Innovation and sense of team rewarded. Sense of excitement and support for risk taking.

Atmosphere

Motive to be productive is high because security depends on your value.

Key Ingredients For Survival/Success

Skill

This is like wearing shoes when you go to work. You must have the technical and people skills required for the job and must always be involved in continuous learning.

Culture

You must know not only what your job is but how it fits with what is valued and rewarded in the organization. What are the unspoken do's and taboos?

A Helping Hand

The old adage should really say, "It is **WHAT** you know <u>and</u> **WHO** you know." It is critical to have a mentor who can give you a hand up and a network to keep you informed.

Agility

With the rapid changes in today's workplace, the capacity for flexibility and creativity are a must. Managing change successfully is a survival strategy.

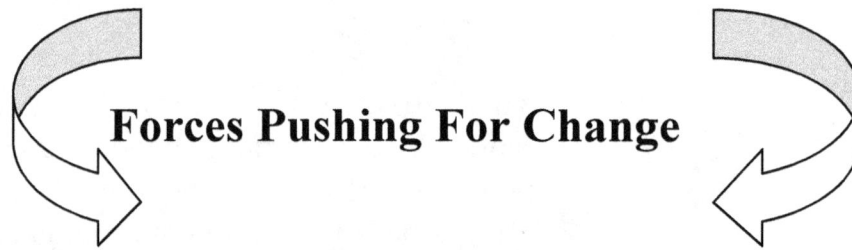

Forces Pushing For Change

Customer
Customers are not accepting what and how we give them goods and services. With mass media, they have raised their level of awareness and standards for consumption.

Competition
Decreasing governmental controls and global competition have broadened who we measure ourselves against.

Orchestration
Technology has made many things obsolete and opened numerous opportunities.

Change
Change is pervasive and consistent. Change is not something with a beginning and an end. It is a constant.

These factors have created a new environment for business. The old rules and tools simply do not apply.

Ten Principles of Entrepreneurial Organizations

1. Steer -- Don't row.

2. Don't just deliver -- Empower.

3. Competition vs. Monopoly

4. Remember the mission, not the rules.

5. Outcomes are more important than inputs.

6. Sustain the customers' needs, not the bureaucracy's.

7. Focus on earning, not spending.

8. Prevention is better than cure.

9. Get authority to the most efficient levels.

10. Leverage change through the market, not just more programs.

Barriers to Successful Change

1) **Fuzzy Vision** -- People do not clearly understand where the organization wants to end up. People do not understand the why of the change.

2) **Lack of Conviction in the Change** -- Key people do not believe the change will be positive in the long run. In the past there has been lots of rhetoric about change but nothing has happened, or change has been poorly implemented in the past.

3) **Ignoring Normal Resistance** -- Resistance is a natural response to change. Even if people want the change, they will not like the uncertainty or disruption it causes. This is particularly dangerous with middle managers because they have to lead the process.

4) **Failure to Communicate Clearly** -- This is the time to manage and direct communication as clearly as possible. For example, A. H. Robbins created a "Rumor Line" when they were undergoing massive change. IBM has established a Dear Abby type column in their newsletter directed at CEO.

5) **No Rewards or Consequences** -- People will not take new ways of doing things seriously unless they understand how they will benefit from adapting or how they will suffer for not doing so.

6) **Lack of Tolerance for Errors** -- If an organization has historically rewarded low risk-taking by punishing mistakes and not rewarding innovation, this will be a hard paradigm shift.

7) **Lack of Orchestration** -- It is important to see the whole picture and seeing how the different pieces will fit together. Remember the "white space."

8) **Lack of Persistence** -- Large-scale organizational change requires a lengthy time commitment and constant readjustment and re-evaluation.

Keys To Making Organizational Change Work

<u>Instructions</u>: The following are key elements to helping organizations succeed in change. Check the ones you think exist in your organization.

_____ 1) We have a good reason to do it.

_____ 2) Person(s) leading the change are respected and valued by those that have to be a part of the change.

_____ 3) The people involved in the change are part of the planning and implementation.

_____ 4) We are creating cross-functional groups that can anticipate and work out problems that will emerge.

_____ 5) We are training people about what new ways of behaving or new values that are desired.

_____ 6) We have pictured the change through new logos, new words, new traditions or other visible means.

_____ 7) We acknowledge resistance and confusion as normal.

_____ 8) We have celebrated incremental achievements and stopped to reflect on how much has already been done.

_____ 9) We have used outside help to clarify our vision, keep us focused and reinforce our position.

_____ 10) We recognize that in today's environment we are looking at continuous change. We reward flexibility, adaptation and agility rather than loyalty, seniority and not making waves.

Key Players in Change

1) **Sponsors**   Those who have the power to legitimize a change.

2) **Agents**   The people who actually make the change happen, carry it out.

3) **Targets**   The people who have to make the changes.

4) **Advocates**   These are people who advocate the change but do not have the power in the organization to sponsor it.

5) **Challengers**   Those brave enough to ask questions and disagree.

- You can be all of these at one time or another.

- In your agency's current situation, what role can you play?

- Think of a current change you want to make. Whose name can you put next to each category?

Sponsor _____

Agent _____

Target _____

Advocate _____

Challenger _____

Force Field Analysis

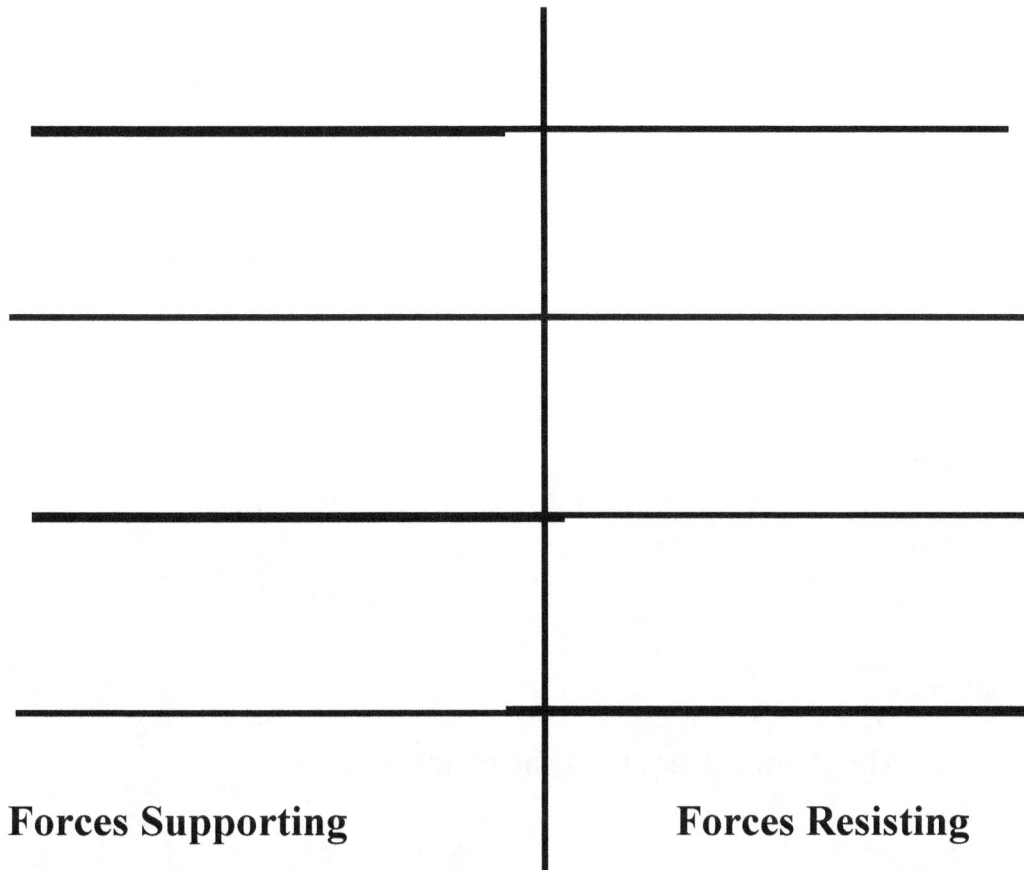

Forces Supporting

Forces Resisting

Status Quo
(Remaining the Same)

Considering A Current Change

1) For me, the most urgent part of the change process I need to attend to is . . .

2) In order for this change to be successful, I need to . . .

3) I need to stop . . . in order for this process to work.

4) My greatest fear about the changes is . . .

5) My boss can help me buy into this by . . .

6) My coworkers can help me by . . .

Action Plan

1) What am I going to tell my boss I learned here today?

2) What can I share with my coworkers about what I learned today?

3) What is one thing I can do differently right away?

Bad Energy

Scenario #1

Jason has always been somewhat negative, but the team puts up with his whining because basically he is a hard worker and has a good heart. Since the Department Head announced some of the changes that will be happening, he has been difficult to be around—so much that when he is not in the office, the mood is considerably more positive. People keep trying to avoid him at all costs, and it is beginning to affect team communication.

Today, apparently your boss, Tonya, had a chat with him, because when you got back from the warehouse, he cornered you and started ranting about how Tonya wants him to "pretend everything is just perfect."

How do you respond? As a team member but not a "boss," what can you do to help?

Not Listening

Scenario #2

Maria is a new supervisor to your team. She came from another organization in Arizona and has a lot of ideas of how "things can be improved." She is bright, and you know she means well, but she is irritating her whole team, and from what you hear from her peers they too are fed up with the "back in Arizona..." thing.

You work well together, and one day both of you are alone in the office early. She catches you off guard when she asks you, "What am I doing wrong? I am trying hard to make some much needed changes here. That is why I was hired. I like the people and think this group can reach the same level of production my old group had. You have been around for a long time and people trust you. Any suggestions?"

What do you respond? Is this an appropriate question? How can you be helpful?

Waste of Time

Scenario #3

Barb is on a committee with you designed to make some recommendations to management regarding ways to cut costs. You have no idea why she volunteered for the committee because she shows up late, doesn't complete her assignments, and just in general doesn't seem to take it seriously.

Several people in the group have asked you to talk to her since the two of you have known each other for a while.

Another team member tried to approach her publicly last week, and she said, "Who do they think they are kidding? This committee is a waste of time and just a way for management to tell the Board they had staff input." You do not agree with her.

How would you approach this?

The Rumors

Scenario #4

Every time there is an article in the paper about the organization, John goes into crazy speculations regarding lay-offs, outsourcing, and other catastrophic scenarios. He feeds the rumors, and as a co-worker you find the whole thing upsetting. There is enough real stuff going on without the rumors and catastrophizing John stirs up.

What can you do? How do rumors affect a change effort? How have you seen rumors dealt with effectively?

Additional Resources

Adams, Marilee. <u>Change Your Questions, Change Your Life</u>. San Francisco: Barrett-Koehler Publishers, 2004.

Altschuler, Alan and Robert D. Behn. <u>Innovation In American Government</u>. Washington, DC: Brookings Institute Press, 1997.

Bardwick, Judith. <u>Danger in the Comfort Zone</u>. New York: AMACOM, 1991.

Block, Peter. <u>The Empowered Manager</u>. San Francisco: Jossey-Bass, 1987.

Block, Peter. <u>Stewardship</u>. San Francisco: Berrett-Koehler, 1993.

Buckingham, Marcus. <u>Go Put Your Strengths to Work</u>. New York: Simon and Schuster, 2007.

Hammond, Sue Annis. <u>The Thin Book of Appreciative Inquiry</u>. Bend, Oregon: Thin Book Publishing, 1996.

Hammond, Sue Annis, and Andrea B. Mayfield. <u>Naming the Elephants</u>. Bend, Oregon: Thin Book Publishing, 2004.

Kotter, John P. and Dan S. Cohen. <u>The Heart of Change</u>. Boston, Mass.: Harvard Businesss School Press, 2002

Linden, Russell M. <u>Seamless Government</u>. San Francisco: Jossey-Bass, 1994. (Also has workbook published in 1998 in paperback.)

Osborne, David and Ted Gaebler. <u>Reinventing Government</u>. Reading: Addison Wesley, 1992.

Patterson, Kerry, Joseph Grenny, Ron McMillan, and Al Switzler. <u>Crucial Conversations</u>. New York: McGraw-Hill, 2002.

Managing Change
PRE- AND POST-TEST

<u>Directions</u>: Please circle the correct answer. If you do not know the answer, you may check "Do not know."

1. The strongest motivator to get people to change is...

   a) potential gain or advantage
   b) pain or discomfort
   c) education around why change is needed
   d) Do not know.

2. A paradigm is...

   a) a tough decision
   b) a mistake that needs correcting
   c) a way of looking at things
   d) Do not know.

3. The first stage/phase in an organization's response to change is...

   a) anger
   b) disbelief or denial
   c) challenging
   d) Do not know.

4. The most important of the key players in a change process is/are the...

   a) sponsor
   b) advocates
   c) targets
   d) Do not know.

5. A 'Force Field Analysis' is...

   a) a statistical way to analyze change
   b) a way to weigh the elements helping to change and the elements getting in the way
   c) a way to justify why you need to change
   d) Do not know.

Managing Change
PRE- AND POST-TEST

<u>Directions</u>: Please circle the correct answer. If you do not know the answer, you may circle "Do not know."

1. The strongest motivator to get people to change is...

    a) potential gain or advantage
    b) pain or discomfort
    c) education around why change is needed
    d) Do not know.

2. A paradigm is...

    a) a tough decision
    b) a mistake that needs correcting
    c) a way of looking at things
    d) Do not know.

3. The first stage/phase in an organization's response to change is...

    a) anger
    b) disbelief or denial
    c) challenging
    d) Do not know.

4. The most important of the key players in a change process is/are the...

    a) sponsor
    b) advocates
    c) targets
    d) Do not know.

5. A 'Force Field Analysis' is...

    a) a way to force change
    b) a way to weigh the elements helping to change and the elements getting in the way
    c) a way to discourage change
    d) Do not know.

Understanding Your Role in Change and Being an Effective Change Agent in Your Organization's Culture

September 2009

Presented by

Carol Susan DeVaney, CPF, CPLP
DeVaney-Wong International, LLC

For Your Notes

OBJECTIVES

Day #1

1. Learn practical tips for how to effectively lead a change effort

2. Understand the key dynamics for building effective relationships that get things done

3. Understand the importance of understanding organizational culture and political savvy in making things work

Day #2

1. Understand the basics of the strategic plan

2. Review basic elements of planning

3. Explore the day to day relevance of the organizations strategic plan and its design

4. Understand the development of a business case or a provocative proposition

5. Look at positive ways to have input into the planning process

AGENDA

Day #1

Introductions

- ➤ What Motivates Change
- ➤ Understanding How Individuals Respond to Change
- ➤ Elements of Successful Change
- ➤ Common Pitfalls
- ➤ The Power of Relationships

Day #2

- ➤ Phases in Organizational Transition
- ➤ Performance Audit
- ➤ Strategic Planning
- ➤ The business case or the provocative proposition
- ➤ Summary and evaluation

Pain or Gain

There are only two reasons why organizations or individuals undergo a change process

Current or Anticipated **PAIN**

Current or Anticipated **GAIN**

So a fundamental question you must ask yourself about every member of your team is "why would they want to do things differently?"

Common Reactions Individuals Have to Change

1. People will feel awkward, ill at ease and self-conscious.

   Like being a fish in a bowl.

2. People will be concerned about what they have to give up -- loss.

   It is unlikely they will first think of what might be gained.

3. People will be concerned they don't have enough time, money or resources.

   Perhaps more critical they fear loosing their status as experts   and being in a learner role.

4. People can handle only so much change at a time.

5. People are ready for and react to change differently. Some jump in and soon run out of steam, while others gradually increase momentum.

6. People will feel alone even if everyone else is going through the change.

7. As soon as the pressure is off, there is a tendency to want things to go back to how they were.

DON'T LET CHANGE
KNOCK YOU OFF YOUR FEET

Tip Sheet for Coping with Change

1. Give yourself permission to be in a learning posture. We all need time to understand and adjust to change.

2. Keep a check on your anticipatory anxiety. Often the anticipation of the unknown is more stressful than the actual event.

3. Focus on what you want not on what you fear.

4. Sort out what you can and can't control. Try to keep yourself in a position where you can make some of the choices even if they are small ones.

5. Get help. Others may not realize you need help, or they may not know what kind of help you need.

6. Don't compare yourself to others who are going through similar situations. They can be a great source of support, but everyone does not react the same to risk and ambiguity.

7. Take time out to recharge. Sometimes we get so involved in the change process we lose total perspective on the situation.

8. It is a struggle to leave the old behind, but in doing so, we face new experiences and opportunities.

9. Give yourself credit. You did not get to the age you are without having some success at managing change. Review those successes and make them work for you.

10. Give others credit. Success tends to generate success.

Breaking Old Assumptions
in the Workplace

Loyalty & Security

Traditional LOYALTY assumes a reciprocal dependent relationship. I, the worker, am loyal to you and you in turn will take care of me = SECURITY

Hierarchy vs Flatness

The supervisor/employee ratio makes leading by position very difficult. Employees need to make decisions at lower levels to be responsive to time and customer pressures.

Seniority & Continuous Learning

The assumption that seniority gave us a special edge is being challenged since skills are becoming obsolete in much shorter increments.

The worker who is keeping up not only with current but also with emerging technologies is now prized. This worker may not have as much "experience" or age.

For the first time in our history we have four distinct generations in the workplace.

Incremental vs Constant Change

Customer demands, global competition and constantly changing technology do not always allow the luxury of incremental change.

Those who can see constant turmoil as the way business will be done, and not as a temporary phenomenon, will survive. Agility is seen as key to survival.

PARADIGMS

1. What are some of the negative paradigms that exist about your organization or your department?

2. What are some paradigms that negatively affect my office? My team?

3. What are some paradigms I am operating under that may not be effective?

4. What can I do to challenge assumptions?

ORGANIZATIONAL REACTIONS TO CHANGE

DENIAL/DISBELIEF

People act as if nothing is happening. There is a general numbness. There is apathy and a sense of "this too will pass." Disbelief that "they really mean" the change. Focus is on the past and you see lots of activity but little end result or a shutting down.
The most important task for the manager is to confront the individuals with truthful information. Let them know the change will happen, what is expected from them and how they can prepare themselves.

Worst thing to do: Bring in a motivational speaker or celebrate.

RESISTANCE/SADNESS

Here you see anger, disappointment and opposition. Groups round up the wagons; lack of cooperation. There is a sense of generalized negativity. Here you may see accidents, absenteeism, illnesses and general acting out.
The most important task for the manager is to allow the feelings to emerge and to manage the conflict. People who had been competently self assured may be unsettled.

Worst thing to do: Not allow people the opportunity to express apprehensions, fears, concerns.

LEARNING CURVE/ANXIETY

People begin to try new things. As a manager this can be an overwhelming time because people deluge you with new ideas and suggestions and you might even feel like your authority is challenged. The group feels like there is too much to do and not a clear focus or direction. You see people slowly beginning to accept the change but many are anxious about the new skills they must learn.
The task for the manager here is to help set goals, help prioritize and help facilitate problem solving.

Worst thing to do: Not allow for mistakes. We are never experts at something new. Reward steps in the right direction. Don't wait for complete success to reward. Recognize that formal training may be needed.

THE WAY IT IS

People begin to see the change as "the way it is." They begin to actively participate and contribute to the change. You see people initiating their work again and individuals begin to become teams again.
The task of the manager is to facilitate "team building." Folks are settling into new roles and ways of doing things and old team patterns and norms may not apply.

Worst thing to do: Slack off and assume it is finished. Do not be surprised when people slide back. It is important that you keep consistently focused on where you want to go.

PHASES IN AN ORGANIZATION'S LIFE CYCLE

Start Up
Few people, long hours. Rules being made up as needed. Salaries usually not good. Lots of unknowns but room for creativity.

Rapid Growth
Rapid growth and customer demands. Loose structure and people take on multiple roles. Much uncertainty. Thin line between success and chaos. Constant need for more/different resources.

Structure
Growth begins to stabilize and formal structure gets put in place to manage it. Employees begin to have some longevity and the organization has a clear sense of history.

Maturation
Distinct established culture. Lots of structure and procedures. Implementing change is more difficult because boundaries are more rigid.   What has made them successful in the past can hurt their future.

Change can be needed at

ANY or ALL

of the phases

KEYS TO MAKING ORGANIZATIONAL CHANGE WORK

Instructions: The following are key elements to helping organizations succeed in change. On a scale of 1 to 7 with 1 being poor and 7 being excellent, how well are you attending to these elements?

_____1. We have good reason to do it.

_____2. Person(s) leading the change are respected and valued by those that have to be a part of the change.

_____3. The key folks in the change process have been included in planning and execution design.

_____4. We are creating cross-functional groups that can anticipate and work out problems that will emerge.

_____5. We are coaching and training people on the skills and attitudes that will be needed.

_____6. We have pictured the change through new logos, new words, new traditions, and other visible means at the right time in the process.

_____7. We acknowledge resistance and confusion as normal. It is unlikely everyone will be on board at the same time.

_____8. We have celebrated steps in the right direction and hitting early wins.

_____9. We have used outside help, when needed, to clarify our vision, keep us focused, and reinforce our position.

_____10. We recognize that in today's environment we are looking at continuous change. We reward flexibility, adaptation, and agility rather than loyalty, seniority, and not making waves.

ORGANIZATIONAL CLIMATE

Think about the current assessment climate in the organization you are trying to help change. Check **characteristics** which apply.

_____1. People avoid taking risks

_____2. People are cynical

_____3. Nobody wants to own up to any problems

_____4. Mistakes are seen as a necessary part of learning

_____5. There is a sense that how well you perform matters

_____6. People are rigid about rules and policies

_____7. Accountability is low

_____8. Not making mistakes is valued more than how well you perform

_____9. Everyone feels they are under attack

___10. People feel that they are valued by the team

___11. The atmosphere seems chaotically busy but not necessarily productive

___12. New ideas and disagreements are accepted

Organizational Climate Scoring:

Put a check mark next to the statement numbers from the assessment.

Entitlement Atmosphere

_____1

_____6

_____7

_____8   Total _____

High Threat Atmosphere

_____2

_____3

_____9

_____11   Total _____

Performance Based Atmosphere

_____4

_____5

_____10

_____12   Total _____

ORGANIZATIONAL CLIMATE SNAPSHOTS

Entitlement

People avoid taking risks by focusing and adhering to strict rules and policies…lots of red tape. The focus is on not making mistakes rather than performance. There is very little accountability because the focus is on the rule checking, not the outcome.

High Threat

People feel cynical and vulnerable. Trust is low. There is a fear of exposing any problems and people are quick to point fingers when they emerge. There is a lot of stress and chaos but often little to show for it. Everyone is focused on saving themselves and building their little empire.

PERFORMANCE BASED

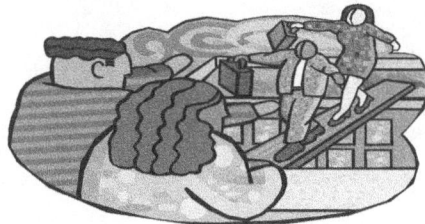

It is clear about its vision and innovation and trying out new things is rewarded. Mistakes are seen as necessary to learning but there are clear accountability expectations. A sense of team is supported because the group's outcomes are rewarded. Change is easier to implement in a performance based climate. What can leaders do to address the challenges in an entitled or a highly fearful environment?

```
┌─────────────────────────┐
│                         │
│   ENTITLEMENT           │
│              ┌──────────┼──────────────┐
│              │          │              │
└──────────────┼──────────┘              │
               │  HIGH THREAT            │
               │      ┌──────────────────┼──────────────┐
               │      │                  │              │
               └──────┼──────────────────┘              │
                      │       PERFORMANCE               │
                      │          BASED                  │
                      │                                 │
                      └─────────────────────────────────┘
```

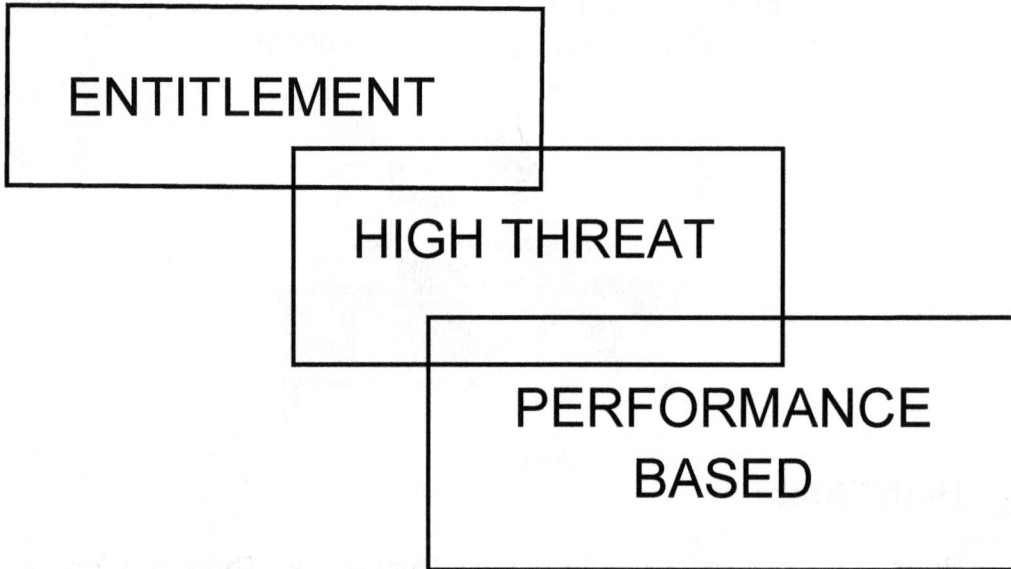

Trust is a key element in a performance based environment.
How can each of us continue to build trust?

KEY INGREDIENTS FOR
ORGANIZATIONAL SURVIVAL/SUCCESS

SKILL	This is like wearing shoes when you go to work. You must have the technical and people skills required for the job and must always be involved in continuous learning.
CULTURE	You must know not only what your job is but how it fits with what is valued and rewarded in the organization. What are the unspoken do's and taboos?
A 360° HELPING HAND	The old adage should really say, "It is WHAT you know and WHO you know." It is critical to have a mentor who can give you a hand up, a network to keep you informed and a support system to help you feel engaged.
AGILITY	With the rapid changes in today's workplace, the capacity for flexibility and creativity are a must. Managing change successfully is a survival strategy.

ASSESSING YOUR STRENGTHS/VULNERABILITY

1. How has the current organizational climate impacted you and your department?

2. What are you currently doing to keep ahead of new advances and expectations?

3. Who are your mentors? Are they appropriate choices?

4. What shape is your network in?

5. What helps you cope with constant change?

ISSUES THAT GET IN THE WAY OF SUCCESSFUL CHANGE

Look at these 8 barriers to successful change. Which have you seen in action?

1. **The Desired End is Not Clear**

   People do not understand where the organization wants to end up. People do not understand the why of the change.

2. **Lack of Conviction in the Change**

   Key people do not believe the change will be positive in the long run. In the past there has been lots of rhetoric about change but nothing has happened, or change has been poorly implemented in the past.

3. **Pretending Nobody Will Oppose the Change**

   Resistance is a natural response to change. Even if people want the change, they will not like the uncertainty or disruption it causes. This is particularly dangerous with middle managers because they have to lead the process.

4. **Failure to Communicate Clearly**

   This is the time to manage and direct communication as clearly as possible.

5. **Not Rewarding the Right Things**

   People will not take new ways of doing things seriously unless they understand how they will benefit from adapting or how they will suffer for not doing so.

6. **Lack of Tolerance for Errors**

   If an organization has historically rewarded low risk-taking by punishing mistakes and not rewarding innovation, this will be a hard paradigm shift.

7. **Lack of Orchestration**

   It is important to see the whole picture and seeing how the different pieces will fit together. Remember the "white space."

8. **Lack of Persistence**

   Large-scale organizational change requires a lengthy time commitment and constant readjustment and re-evaluation

LEVELS OF CHANGE

COSMETIC

This is when you make minor, incremental, cosmetic or simply accommodating changes.

Example
This can be a new logo or marketing focus.

STRUCTURAL

This is when change involves the whole organization. It involves developing new ways of operating.

Example
Going from one to 3 locations.

TRANSFORMATIONAL

Most radical of all change. It is breaking the paradigm. It is sudden and extensive. It redefines what you do and who you are as an organization.

Example
Electric lines vs a new power grid system.

PARADIGMS

1. What are some of the paradigms we are operating under in our organization?

2. What organization would we want to be compared to positively?

3. What is the worst future scenario for our organization?

4. My "ideal" for our organization would be that...

5. My contribution to that ideal would be...

COMMON REASONS FOR CHANGE

From a systems standpoint, no matter what the change is, it will have an effect on the

WHOLE!

CUSTOMER	Customers are not accepting what and how we give them goods and services. With mass media, they have raised their level of awareness and standards for consumption.
COMPETITION	Our competition can often come from unexpected sources.
INNOVATION	New discoveries or new cultural frameworks can make old ways obsolete.
GLOBAL ECONOMY	What happens "THERE" affects us "HERE". What are some other factors that are affecting you?
CHANGE	Change is pervasive and consistent. Change is not something with a beginning or an end. It is a constant.

FORCE FIELD ANALYSIS

Forces Pushing   **Forces Resisting**

Status Quo

(Remaining the Same)

Think of an action or change you want to make. Describe the forces supporting your decision and the forces resisting. What can you do to either increase the support or decrease the resistance?

Alignment and Performance

Alignment requires that we understand how our performance is being measured.

On a score of 1-5 with 1 being "totally disagree" and 5 being "totally agree," how would you rate yourself on the following statements:

_____1.   I understand how the department's mission contributes to the organization's mission.

_____2.   I know how my job contributes to achieving the organization's mission.

_____3.   I can identify areas where we succeeded and failed in 2008.

_____4.   I can understand what I do contributes to the success of the other people in my office.

Ten Key Learning Points
from Strategic Planning Video

The Mission Statement

"The mission statement should be a comprehensive, general, and results-oriented statement that brings the agency into focus, by clearly explaining why it exists and what it does. The statement should be derived at least in part from relevant statutes, such as any authorizing legislation."

Your notes from video…

_____

_____

_____

_____

_____

_____

_____

_____

_____

_____

_____

_____

_____

_____

_____

_____

_____

_____

General Goals and Objectives

"There should be a set of general, long-term (minimum of five years) strategic goals that are clearly derived from the mission statement and are results oriented. Under each goal should be arrayed one or more objectives that are also results oriented and somewhat more specific than the general goals. To the maximum extent possible, these goals and objectives should be outcome oriented, rather than output or process oriented."

Your notes from video…

_____
_____
_____
_____
_____
_____
_____
_____
_____
_____
_____
_____
_____
_____
_____
_____
_____
_____
_____
_____
_____

Strategies to Achieve Goals and Objectives

"There should be a description of how the agency intends to achieve the goals and objectives. This is the 'strategy' part of the strategic plan, and is to include brief descriptions of the operational processes, skills and technology, and the human, capital, information and other resources required to meet those goals and objectives It should cover the overall approach that will be taken over the timeframe, including a schedule for significant actions."

Your notes from video…

_____

_____

_____

_____

_____

_____

_____

_____

_____

_____

_____

_____

_____

_____

_____

_____

_____

_____

_____

_____

External Factors

"There should be an identification of those key factors external to the organization and beyond its control that could significantly affect achievement of any of the general goals and objectives. These may include both governmental and non-governmental factors, but should generally not include as a factor the possible lack of a significant increase in funding. These factors should also not include anything highly unlikely to occur or those that have only a tangential influence on achievement of the goals."

Your notes from video…

_____

_____

_____

_____

_____

_____

_____

_____

_____

_____

_____

_____

_____

_____

_____

_____

_____

_____

Program Evaluations

"In some program areas, the measurement of effectiveness requires an analytic process known as program evaluations. This is an objective and formal assessment of the implementation and results of a program, including its operating policies and practices. The strategic plan should include a description of the program evaluations used in establishing or revising the general goals and objectives, along with a schedule for periodic future program evaluations."

Your notes from video…

_____

_____

_____

_____

_____

_____

_____

_____

_____

_____

_____

_____

_____

_____

_____

_____

_____

_____

_____

_____

Coordination of Cross-Cutting Functions

"Agencies with similar or related goals and objectives should coordinate their efforts in planning, program implementation, and performance measurement. They should not be acting in isolation, but instead should consider how their own programs can synergistically contribute to the effectiveness of the efforts of other agencies."

Your notes from video…

_____
_____
_____
_____
_____
_____
_____
_____
_____
_____
_____
_____
_____
_____
_____
_____
_____
_____
_____
_____
_____

Data Capacity

"In order for effective policy to be made, it is important that the level of program performance be accurate. And in order for effective management to occur, it is important that the performance information be reported on a regular periodic basis throughout the year --- not just at year-end. This need for timely, accurate performance information requires that the agency have effective data capacity. It requires systems to be in place that can track and report performance information that is linked to each of the annual goals and measures, and in turn to the strategic goals and objectives. Program managers, as well as agency executives, need access to this information in order to manage for results."

Your notes from video…

_____

_____

_____

_____

_____

_____

_____

_____

_____

_____

_____

_____

_____

_____

_____

Treatment of Major Management Problems

"The strategic plan should address major weakness in the management of its programs, as well as the high-risk areas identified by GAO, especially as they adversely affect the ability of the agency to achieve its long-term and annual goals."

Your notes from video…

_____

_____

_____

_____

_____

_____

_____

_____

_____

_____

_____

_____

_____

_____

_____

_____

_____

_____

_____

_____

_____

_____

_____

Local Authority and Stakeholder Consultations

"When developing a strategic plan, the agency is required to consult with Congress (i.e., its authorization and appropriation committees), and to solicit and consider the views and suggestions of these entities potentially affected by or interested in such plan. This includes both governmental and non-governmental entities, such as program customers and clients. Development of the plan is not subject to the Administrative Procedure Act, but the agency should attempt to solicit a range of interests for their views." Contrary views regarding the final plan should be summarized (but not individually attributed), and areas of disagreement generalized.

Your notes from video…

_____

_____

_____

_____

_____

_____

_____

_____

_____

_____

_____

_____

_____

_____

_____

The Annual Performance Plan:
Annual Performance Goals and Measures

"The annual performance plan is required to establish performance goals that define the level of performance to be achieved by each program activity in the agency's budget. These goals may in turn be supported by performance measures. The goals and measures should specifically state the level of expected performance, and do so in a manner that provides a basis for subsequent comparison with actual performance. The actual goals should be expressed in an objective, quantifiable, and measurable form unless OMB has approved an alternative form. In addition, the annual plan goals should provide an explicit linkage between the mission statement and general goals and objectives of the strategic plan on the one hand, and the day-to-day activities of each program on the other hand."

Eleven Pitfalls of Strategic Planning and Performance Management

Look at the Strategic Plan. Put a Y (Yes) if you think it successfully avoids the pitfall and an N (No) if it doesn't.

_____1.　A mission statement with elements so broad and general it could apply to other agencies.

_____2.　General goals and objectives that are more process oriented than outcome oriented.

_____3.　Neglecting to solicit input from affected shareholders.

_____4.　Neglecting to use program evaluations to establish goals and strategies.

_____5.　Identifying strategies for achieving the goals which are actually just descriptions of current activities.

_____6.　Weak linkage between strategic goals and annual performance.

_____7.　Inadequate linkage to the budget.

_____8.　Inadequate discussion of external factors.

_____9.　Major management problems not addressed.

_____10.　No coordination of crosscutting functions.

_____11.　Little discussion of what data is needed and how to get it in a timely way.

From GAO and Congressional Evaluators Reports

President's Initiatives

Instructions: How does the organization support these 3 initiatives?

1. Government should be transparent

2. Government should be participatory

3. Government should be collaborative

Strategic Plan

Mission

We provide leadership on food, agriculture, natural resources, and related issued based on sound public policy and the best available science, and efficient management.

Vision

We want to be recognized as a dynamic organization that is able to efficiently provide the integrated program delivery needed to lead a rapidly evolving food and agriculture system.

Can you think of ways to turn this into a

"provocative

Proposition"?

KEY ROLES IN CHANGE

1. **Sponsors**   Those who have the power either in position or resources to legitimize a change.

2. **Advocates**   These are people who advocate the change but do not have the power in the organization to sponsor it.

3. **Agents**   The people who carry it out.

4. **Targets**   The people who will be impacted.

5. **Challengers**   Those brave enough to ask questions and disagree.

ROLES IN CHANGE

❖ You can be all of these at one time or another

❖ In your organization's current situation, what role can you play? Why?

❖ Think of a current change you want to make. Whose name can you put next to each category?

Sponsor   _____

Advocate   _____

Agent   _____

Target   _____

Challenger   _____

STEPS IN CHANGE EXECUTION

The following are 6 questions that can help shape the process for executing the change.

Question # 1
"What is the compelling reason why this change has to happen now?"

Question # 2
"What will success look like if we accomplish it?"

Question # 3
"Who do I need supporting the change and what will their roles be?"

Question # 4
"What is the most effective way to proceed that takes the potential risk that may come with the change into consideration?"

Question # 5
"What do we need to do to make sure we are on the right track towards meeting our goals?"

When you reach your destination it is important to ask one closing question:

Question #6
"Did we succeed as expected and what lessons did we learn for future efforts?"

Question # 1
"What is the compelling reason why this change has to happen now?"

What tasks would you expect to have as a change facilitator during this phase?

What tasks would you expect a leader to have?

Question # 2
"What will success look like if we accomplish it?"

What tasks would you expect to have as a change facilitator during this phase?

What tasks would you expect a leader to have?

Question # 3
"Who do I need supporting the change and what will their roles be?"

What tasks would you expect to have as a change facilitator during this phase?

What tasks would you expect a leader to have?

Question # 4

"What is the most effective way to proceed that takes the potential risk that may come with the change into consideration?"

What tasks would you expect to have as a change facilitator during this phase?

What tasks would you expect a leader to have?

Question # 5

"What do we need to do to make sure we are on the right track towards meeting our goals?"

What tasks would you expect to have as a change facilitator during this phase?

What tasks would you expect a leader to have?

Question # 6
"Did we succeed as expected and what lessons did we learn for future efforts?"

What tasks would you expect to have as a change facilitator during this phase?

What tasks would you expect a leader to have?

CHALLENGES TO STRATEGIC PLANNING
AND MEASURING SUCCESS

1.	A mission statement with elements so broad and general it does not really differentiate your organization from any other one.
2.	General goals and objectives focus more on the how and less on the desired outcome.
3.	Affected stakeholders are not solicited for input.
4.	Goals and strategies are formulated with evaluation measures in mind.
5.	Identifying strategies for achieving the goals which are actually just brainstorming or "laundry lists."
6.	Weak linkage between strategic goals, performance measures and resources available.
7.	Inadequate discussion of external factors that can be impacting the process.
8.	Leadership challenges or conflicts that are not attended to.
9.	Lack of insight into how one system might impact another.
10.	Not enough thought to how quickly the data will provide insight into how successful the process is going and/or whether you even have the capacity to generate and evaluate the data.

FROM THE EMPLOYEE'S POINT OF VIEW

Think of a change process you have recently been a part of or witnessed and answer the following questions.

1. How did the leadership describe the reason for the change?

2. What was done to clarify what the desired results would be?

3. Was the plan to get from point A to point B clear to everyone?

4. Do you think every employee in the organization understood his/her role in making the change happen?

Now go back and describe the leadership behaviors that did or did not make it succeed.

SELLING CHANGE

For you to sell a massive change process, you must have answers to the following questions:

1. Why do we exist at all?

2. What changes are occurring in the nation and locally that are pushing us to change?

3. What is changing in the customers I serve? (How are people perceiving my service or product differently? How is my customer being redefined?)

4. What are the current problems we are having as an organization? (too much red tape, too little authority at a line level, outdated services, financial shortfalls, poor leadership, etc.

5. Why won't waiting or small incremental changes do the trick?

6. What will happen if we do not change?

7. What do we want to look like at the end of the change?

The answers to these questions give you your justification or "case" for change.

SAMPLE SITUATIONS

Bad Energy

SCENARIO #1

Jason has always been somewhat negative, but the team puts up with his whining because basically he is a hard worker and has a good heart. Since the Department Head announced some of the changes that will be happening, he has been difficult to be around – so much that when he is not in the office, the mood is considerably more positive. People keep trying to avoid him at all costs, and it is beginning to affect team communication.

Apparently your boss, Tonya, had a chat with him today, because when you got back from the warehouse, he cornered you and started ranting about how Tonya wants him to "pretend everything is just perfect."

How do you respond? As a team member but not a "boss," what can you do to help?

Not Listening

SCENARIO #2

Maria is a peer and the new supervisor to her team. She came from another division in Arizona and has a lot of ideas of how "things can be improved." She is bright, and you know she means well, but she is irritating her whole team, and from what you hear from your other peers they too are fed up with the "back in Arizona..." thing.

You work well together and one day both of you are alone in the office early. She catches you off guard and asks you, "What am I doing wrong? I am trying hard to make some much needed changes here. That is why I was hired. I like the people and think this group can reach the same level of production my old group had. You have been around for a long time and people trust you. Any suggestions?"

What do you respond? Is this an appropriate question? How can you be helpful?

Waste of Time

SCENARIO #3

Clyde is on a committee with you designed to make some recommendations to management regarding ways to cut costs. You have no idea why he volunteered for the committee because he shows up late, doesn't complete his assignments, and just in general doesn't seem to take it seriously.

Several people in the group have asked you to talk to him since the two of you have known each other for a while.

Another team member tried to approach him publicly last week, and he said, "Who do they think they are kidding? This committee is a waste of time and just a way for management to tell the big shots they had staff input." You do not agree with him.

How would you approach this?

The Rumors

SCENARIO #4

Every time there is an article in the paper about your company, John goes into crazy speculations regarding lay-offs, outsourcing, and other catastrophic scenarios. He feeds the rumors. Both of you are supervisors and you find the whole thing upsetting. There is enough real stuff going on without the rumors and catastrophizing John stirs up.

How do rumors affect a change effort?

As a peer what can you do?

What Is Mine Is Mine

SCENARIO #5

You supervise Marta and Sal. Marta and Sal had always cooperated well with one another, and when one team got in a pinch, the other would help out. Since Tod, the Manager, announced there may be some reductions in your department, you notice Sal has been much less friendly and, several times in meetings when Marta has asked for help, has told her his folks are too busy. Now Marta is turning him down for help. Both have worked well for over ten years and are good people. It is creating bad feelings all around and a couple of times has made whole department look bad.

What can you do?

The Dinosaur

SCENARIO #6

You have been in the department for about 6 months. You are fairly new at management, but the reason you were hired is you have a strong technology background and this department is in need of an update in its equipment and processes.

Jack has been with the department over 25 years and from his past evaluations you can tell he was a high performer and was responsible for several innovations ten years ago. You thought he would be a great help as you implemented these changes, but every time you approach him to serve on a committee or get some training, he tells you he will be retiring soon. You discover that, because of his wife's health problems and his age, it will be unlikely that he would retire any sooner than 5 years from now. You simply cannot wait that long.

What would you do?

We Already Tried That

SCENARIO #7

You are promoted to senior management. The person before you, Sonia, had been hired from the "outside" to make major changes. She was here for over two months and you know she made a lot of change efforts but things always seemed to fall flat before anything was completed.

Folks seemed to be happy about your promotion, but now as you try to make changes the staff laughs and tells you you should know better as it obviously did not work for Sonia. They seem to think that now that you are in charge everything can just go back to the way things were. The fact is the department must make changes.

What can you say to the team?

Bad Idea

SCENARIO #8

The Program is thinking of implementing new software in your department. Your boss is quite excited about it and tells you he expects you to manage a smooth implementation.

As you study the materials, you realize this is just not going to meet the needs of the citizens that use your services. When you approach him about this, he accuses you of not being a team player and trying to find an excuse to get out of work. You are quite offended by his attitude but know he is under a lot of pressure to do this as this is a pet project of the new director who used this software in her old organization. Unfortunately, she came from a much smaller organization.

What can you do?

Out To Pasture

SCENARIO #9

Meilin has been an excellent employee for over 27 years. She has always been interested in new things and has taken plenty of opportunities for professional development. Her new boss has come into the department with some wonderful new ideas and Meilin was excited about helping out.

For some reason her new boss thinks she is retiring soon, but she has no plans to do so. She has noticed every time she volunteers to learn one of the pieces of equipment she is told she has plenty to do and not to worry about it. Meilin is beginning to feel she is being put out to pasture.

What should Meilin do?

Sabotage

SCENARIO #10

Prior to the implementation of the new structure, Tom had been a good performer but was always a little negative and sarcastic about things he did not like. Since some of his job duties got changed, he has been intolerable often in public where not only his staff but customers may overhear him talking about how inefficient the organization is. You tried to ignore him for a while thinking he would get this off his chest and move on, but several months have elapsed and you see no progress. The worst part is he is passing on some of his negativity to a couple of new employees in the department he has been training.

What do you do with Tom?

ACTION PLAN

1. What am I going to tell my boss I learned here the past two days?

2. What am I going to share with my staff about the last two days?

3. What is one thing I can do differently right away?

4. What do I now know I am currently doing right when it comes to managing change?

Reading Resources

Abrashoff, Michael. It's Your Ship. Business Plus, New York, N.Y.; 2002.

Adams, Marilee. Change Your Questions, Change Your Life. Barertt-Koehler Publishers, San Francisco, California; 2004.

Ariely, Dan. Predictably Irrational. New York: Harper Collins, 2005.

Bardwick, Judith. Danger in the Comfort Zone. New York: AMACOM, 1991.

Biech, Elaine. Thriving Trough Change. Alexandria: ASTD Press, 2007

Block, Peter. The Empowered Maager. San Francsco: Jossey-Bass, 1987.

Block, Peter. Stewardship. San Francisco: Berrett-Koehler, 1993l

Buckingham, Marcus. Go Put Your Strengths to Work. Simon and Schuster, New York, N.Y.; 2007.

Dalziel, Murray and S. Schoonouer. Changing Ways. New York: AMACOM, 1988.

Drucker, Peter. Innovation and Entrepreneurship. New York: Harper Business, 1993.

Dubner, Steven and Levitt, Steven. Freaknomics. Collins, NY: Harper Collins, 2005, 2006.

Feltman, Charles. The Thin Book of Trust. Bend: Thin Book Publishing, 2009.

Gladwell, Malcolm. Outliers. Little-Brown and Co., New York 2008

Hammer, Michael and J. Champy. Reengineering the Corporation. New York: Harper and Row, 1985.

Hammond, Sue Annis. The Thin Book of Appreciative Inquiry. Thin Book Publishing, Bend, Oregon; 1996.

Hammond, Sue Annis and Andrea B. Mayfield. Naming the Elephants. Thin Book Publishing, Bend, Oregon; 2004.

Hiatt, Jeffrey M., ADKAR. Prosci Learning Center Publications, Lovelan, Colorado, 2006.

Imai, Masaaki. Kaizen. New York: McGraw-Hill, 1986.

Kanter, D. and P. Mirrus. The Cynical American. San Francisco: Jossey-Bass, 1989.

Kanter, Rosabeth Moss. The Change Masters. New York, Simon and Schuster, 1983.

Klein, Kim. Fund Raising for Social Change. Jossey-Bass, San Francisco, California; 2007

Kotter, John P., and Dan S. Cohen. The Heart of Change. Harvard Business School Press, Boston, Massachusetts; 2002.

Kotter, John P. Leading Change. Harvard Business School Press, Boston, Massachusetts; 1996.

Kouzes, James and Barry Z. Posner. The Leadership Challenge. San Francisco: Jossey-Bass, 1995.

Linden, Russell M. Seamless Government. San Francisco: Jossey Bass, 1988.

Morgan, Gareth. Riding the Waves of Change. San Francisco: Jossey-Bass. 1988.

Nadler, David, Marc Gerstein and Robert Shaw. Organizational Architecture. San Francisco: Jossey-Bass, 1992.

Naisbitt, John and Patricia Aburdene. Reinventing the Corporation. New York: Warner Books, 1985.

Osborne, David and Ted Gaebler. Reinventing Government. Reading: Addison Wesley, 1992.

Patterson, Kerry, Joseph Grenny, Ron McMillan, and Al Switzler. Crucial Confrontations. McGraw-Hill, New York, N.Y.; 2002.

Patterson, Kerry, Joseph Grenny, Ron McMillan, and Al Switzler. Crucial Confrontations. McGraw-Hill, New York, N.Y.; 2005.

Peters, Tom. <u>Thriving on Chaos</u>. New York: Harper-Collins, 1992.

Rath, Tom. <u>Vital Friends</u>. New York: Gallup Press, 2006.

Ryan, Kathleen and D. Oestreich. <u>Driving Fear Out of the Workplace</u>. San Francisco: Jossey-Bass, 1991.

Shiller, Robert. <u>Animal Spirits</u>. Princeton, NJ: Princeton University Press, 2009

Thompson, Charles. <u>What a Great Idea</u>. New York: Harper-Collins, 1992.

Tichy, Noel and M.A. Devanna. <u>The Transformational Manager</u>. New York: John   Wiley, 1987.

Websites to Explore

<u>www.whitehous.gov</u>

<u>www.gao.gov</u>

<u>www.govinfo.library.unt.edu</u> (old but still useful)

www.usda.gov

Change Management

Ability to understand institutional aspects and formulate integrated change proposals, which generate a positive influence on sectoral modernization and transformation processes

Competency Elements and Behaviors

1. Understanding of Political Economy

Ability to systematically analyze a country's cultural, political, and institutional environment in order to identify issues which support or limit change processes.

Solid Behaviors: Analyses the institutional and sector environments. Identifies information regarding the reasons for change, actors, and institutional factors and makes recommendations to the team.

Advanced Behaviors: Identifies elements that support and constrain change processes. Analyzes institutional factors, impacts, risks, and the country's political economy. Clarifies the objectives of the change process. Identifies gaps between the current and desired situation. Develops viable scenarios.

Expert Behaviors: Promotes understanding of the regional political economy and institutions. Facilitates dialogue on institutional issues at the highest levels. Builds a shared understanding of the opportunities and barriers for sector modernization processes. Anticipates needs for change.

2.   Change Proposal Development

Ability to formulate change proposals taking into consideration key institutional issues, and to promote politically and technically feasible agreements.

Solid Behaviors: Supports the development of change proposals. Maintains updated methodologies and tools for managing change. Develops technical analysis to close identified gaps in technology, processes, resources, standards, structures, incentives, etc. Develops components of the change plan.

Advanced Behaviors: Formulates comprehensive change proposals. With key actors stakeholders defines change strategies that respond to institutional needs (diagnostics, communication plans, training plans, etc.). Integrates technical and political factors. Creates partnerships with key stakeholders. Makes concessions according to reality without sacrificing the quality of solutions of processes objectives.

Expert Behaviors: Leads the design of sector change proposals. Is recognized as an expert in methodologies and tools for managing change. Conducts high level dialogue on issues of change management. Gets support from key stakeholders for sector transformation processes. Advises on the incorporation of change strategies in sector operations.

3. Implementation of Institutional and Sector Change Strategies

Solid Behaviors: Supports the implementation of change strategies. Assists the counterpart with implementation of actions included in the change plan (communication plan, training, etc.). Supports the definition of functions and activities to be implemented by change agents.

Advanced Behaviors: Advises on the implementation of change strategies. Obtains the support of formal and informal leaders for the implementation of actions. Advises the counterpart, creating trust, and respect. Anticipates divergence from plans and suggests adjustments that address the reality of the country and project. Conducts self effectively in complex political situations.

Expert Behaviors: Leads the implementation of sector change strategies. Is solicited by countries to provide advice on institutional issues that support change and sector modernization processes. Aligns change efforts with countries' developmental goals. Helps solve complex institutional problems. Verifies the effectiveness of change strategies on the project and sector levels.

Remember These?

Home, home on the range,
Where the deer and the antelope play.
Where seldom is heard a discouraging word,
And the skies are not cloudy all day.

Twinkle, twinkle, little star
How I wonder what you are.
Up above the world so high.
Like a diamond in the sky.
Twinkle, twinkle little star.

Mary had a little lamb,
Little lamb, little lamb.
Mary had a little lamb.
Its fleece was white as snow.

Yankee Doodle went to town riding on a pony.
Stuck a feather in his hat and called it macaroni.
Yankee Doodle, keep it up.
Yankee Doodle Dandy.

Row, row, row your boat
Gently down the stream
Merrily, merrily, merrily,
Life is but a dream

The itsy bitsy spider
Crawled up the water spout.
Down came the rain
and washed the spider out.
Out came the sun and dried up all the rain,
And the itsy bitsy spider
Crawled up the spout again.

Happy birthday to you
Happy birthday to you.
Happy birthday dear tear
Happy birthday to you!

If you're happy and you know it clap your hands.
If you're happy and you know it clap your hands.
If you're happy and you know it, then your face will clearly show it.
If you're happy and you know it clap your hands.

Old MacDonald had a farm,
Ei I ee I oh!
And on his farm he had some pigs.
Ei I ee I oh!
With an oink-oink here.
And an oink-oink there
Here an oink, there an oink
Everywhere an oink-oink.
Old MacDonald had a farm,
Ei I ee I oh!

Take me out to the ball game.
Take me out with the crowd.
Buy me some peanuts and Crackerjacks.
I don't care if I never get back.
Let me root, root, root for the home team.
If they don't win it's a shame.
For it's one, two, three strikes you're out
At the old ball game!

London Bridge is falling down,
Falling down, falling down.
London Bridge is falling down,
My fair lady!

DIVERSITY
and
INCLUSION

DIVERSITY & INCLUSION

Diversity & Inclusion As A Change Initiative

Facilitated by

Carol Susan DeVaney, CPF, CPLP
DeVaney-Wong International

OBJECTIVES

Participants will...

- learn SHRM's definitions
- understand creating culture of inclusion requires skills in change management
- elements for successful change
- ideas from other organizations
- resource list

AGENDA

Introductions

SHRM's Definitions

Inclusion as a Cultural
Change Process

Keys to Successful Change

Ideas for Future Action

DIVERSITY

refers to the similarities and differences between individuals accounting for all aspects of one's personal and individual identity.

INCLUSION

provides the potential
for greater innovation
and creativity.

Inclusion
is what enables
organizations to
realize the business
benefits of this potential.

"The Diversity Discipline"

deals with the qualities, experiences and work styles that make individuals unique as well as how organizations can leverage those qualities in support of business objectives.

The <u>Business Case</u> for diversity is the organization's statement of why working on diversity and inclusion align directly with the organization's key business objectives.

In change management
language, we call this the
provocative proposition
or the compelling vision.

Pain / Gain?

Pushing Resisting

The facts of the matter are that of all the frequently asked questions about diversity the four main ones remain focused around the issues of gender, race, age, and opportunity rather than questions of ROI and business imperatives.

DIVERSITY

Awareness

Choices

Change

Organizations' Reactions to Change

1. Denial/Disbelief

2. Anger/Loss

3. Trial and Error

4. Integration/
Institutionalization

Resources
for
Future
Action

THANKS!!

Mastering Diversity and Inclusion

Presented by

Carol Susan DeVaney, CPF, CPLP
DeVaney-Wong International

OBJECTIVES

Participants will:

- Understand how feeling included contributes to team and organizational effectiveness.

- Understand how sameness leads to improvement and diversity leads to innovation and abundance.

- Recognize the value of mutualism as a strategy for innovation and successful teams.

- Learn models for effective cross-cultural communication and understanding.

AGENDA

Introductions/Objectives

Defining Inclusion

A Model for Cross-Cultural
Communication and
Understanding

The Concept of Mutualism

Reaching Common Ground

Ideas Into Practice

Closing

Definitions

EEO

Affirmative Action

Diversity

Inclusion

Perceptions
+
Decisions We Make About Them

= Behavior

=Consequences

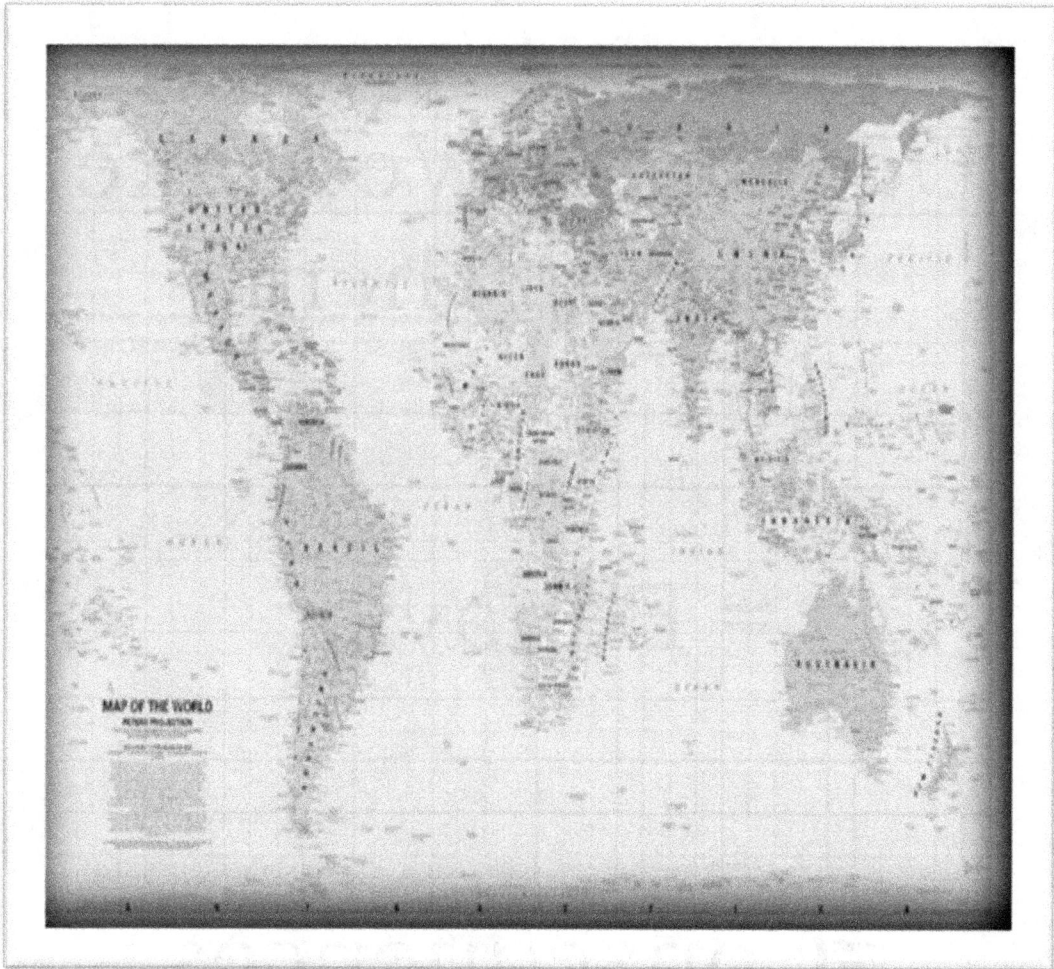

MAP OF THE WORLD
PETER PROJECTION

Compare Europe to South America

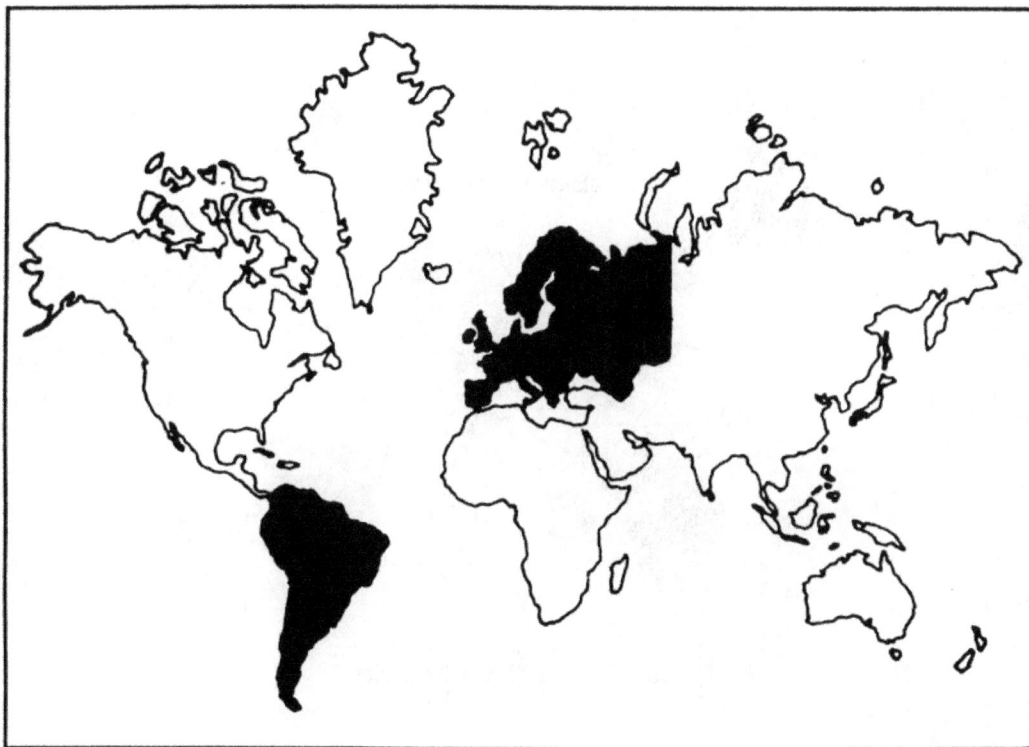

In reality Europe is smaller

Europe: **3.8** mill.sq.miles

South America: **6.9** mill.sq.miles

Compare Africa to former Soviet Union

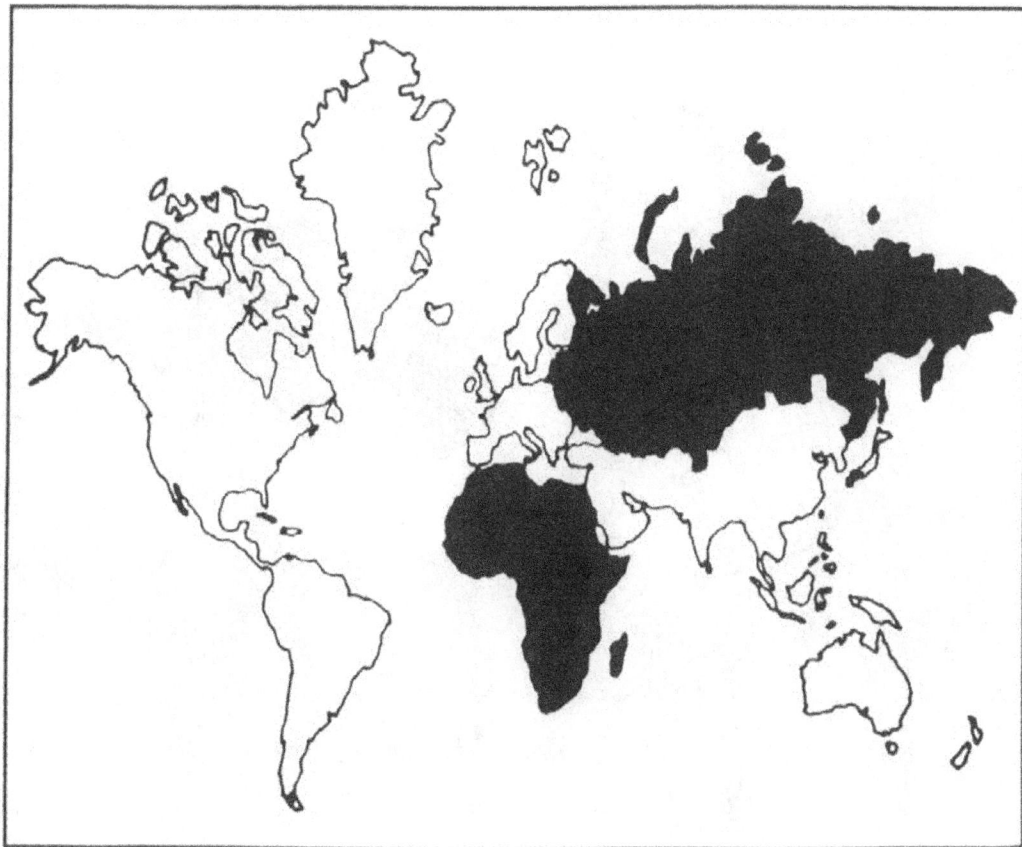

Africa is much larger

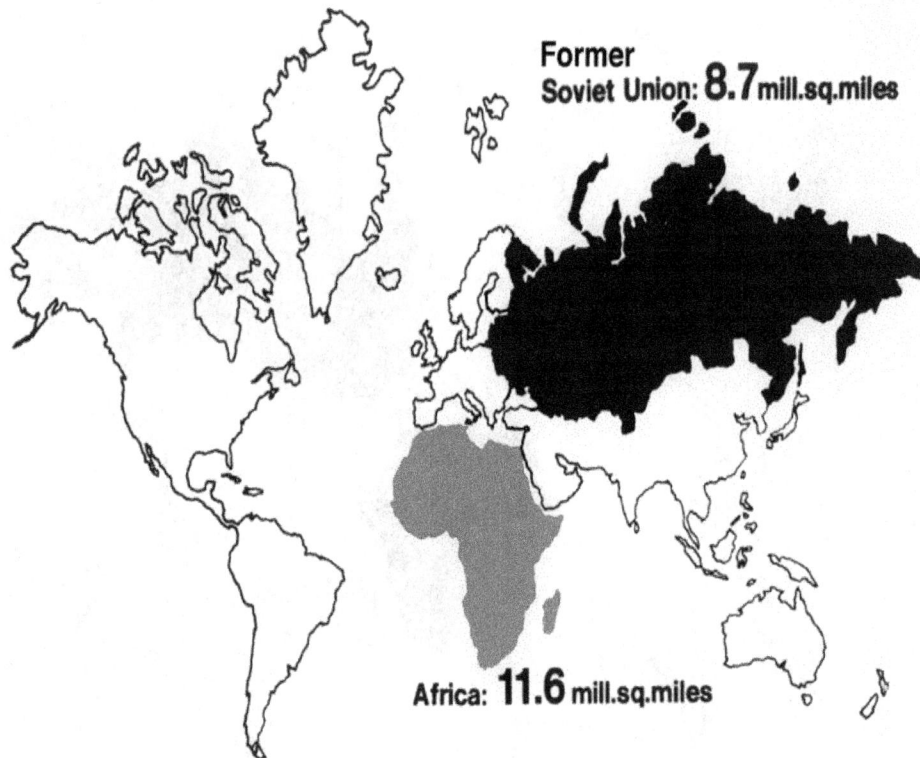

Former Soviet Union: **8.7** mill.sq.miles

Africa: **11.6** mill.sq.miles

Compare Scandinavia to India

Scandinavia: 0.4 mill.sq.miles

India: 1.3 mill.sq.miles

BRIDGING CULTURES
A Model

What I Know

⇩

**What I Think
I Need To Know**

⇩

**What I Don't Even
Know I Should Know**

Stages of Growth Away From

Ethnocentrism

NAÏVE/NO SOCIAL CONSCIOUSNESS

Basically this is when an individual is not even aware that they are part of a group with specific values, norms, and ways of behaving.

ACCEPTANCE

This is when an individual
is aware of a group's
culture and buys into it.

RESISTANCE

This happens when the premises of the individual's group culture are challenged. It is usually met with what appears as a hostile, militant, or over-sensitive response.

REDEFINITION

This is when an individual is willing to question and look beyond the negative stereotypes his group may have had about other groups.

Building Bridges

This is when the person looks for ways to communicate with others outside of his group.

FACTS
TO
KNOW

U.S. CENSUS DATA

White	75.1%
African American	12.3%
American Indian/ Alaskan Native	0.9%
Asian	3.6%
Native Hawaiian/ Pacific Islander	2.6%
Other Race	5.5%
Two or more Races	2.4%
White/Not Hispanic	69.1%
Hispanic	12.5%

Inclusion
A Change Process

Awareness   Choice

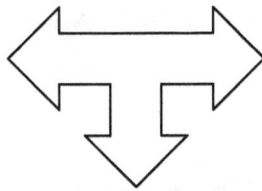

CHANGE

Four Workplace Competencies

SKILL

CULTURAL SAVVY

HAND UP

AGILITY

MENTORING

An agreed-upon relationship
between a senior individual
(mentor) and a junior employee
(protégé) in which the mentor
functions as

sponsor	coach
guide	teacher
ally	catalyst
advocator	supporter
and	role model

to enhance the professional
growth and career
advancement of the protégé.

CHANGES IN WORKPLACE CULTURE

Loyalty   vs   Security
Seniority vs   vs   Performance

Specialization vs Agility
Hierarchy vs Contribution

QUESTIONS TO PONDER
?????????????

Intelligence? ➡️ Traditional IQ

Common Sense
& Self Awareness? ➡️ Emotional
Intelligence

Ability to work with ➡️ Social
and through others? Intelligence

WHAT MOTIVATES THEM?

Support? Skill? Desire?

Two Reasons People Are Willing to Change Their Behavior

PAIN

GAIN

What's In It For Me?

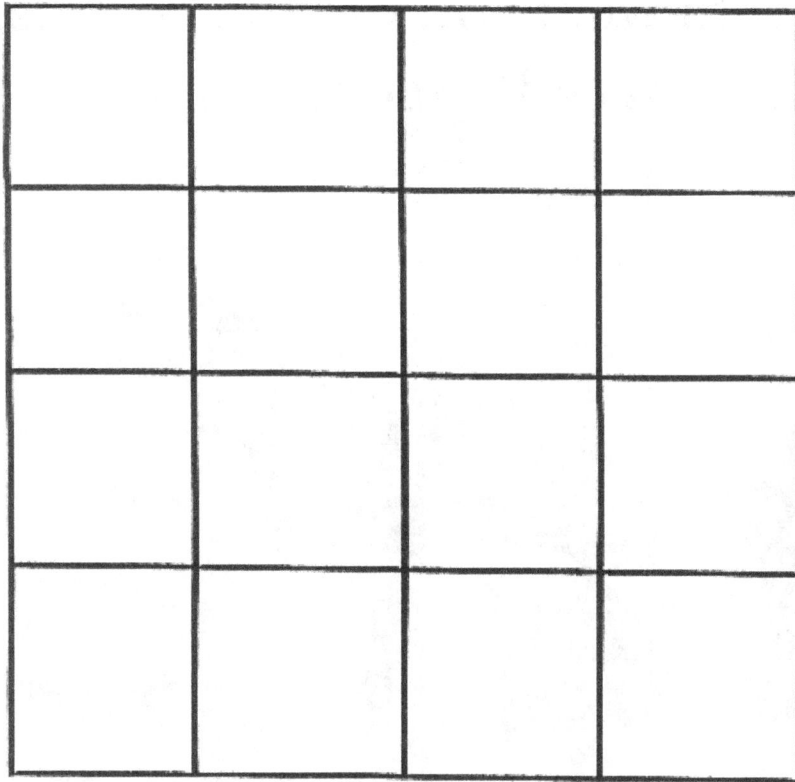

HOW MANY SQUARES DO YOU SEE?

#_____

Start with what you have in common
and work your way out

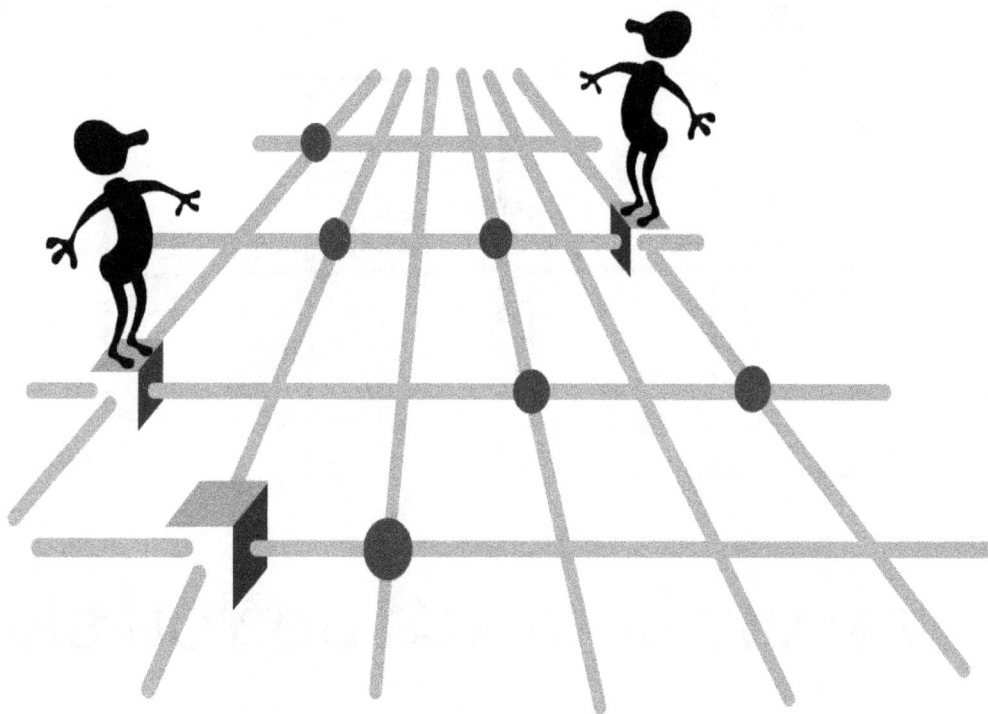

Straight Talk

Straight Talk is communication skills you can use to encourage open, honest, and direct conversation without putting anybody down, especially if someone has said something insensitive, thoughtless, or hostile.

1. Description correction

2. Check the content

3. Repeat the statement

4. Expletives or accents

5. Comparative relationship

6. Challenge

7. "I" message

8. Direct statement

9. Peer Modeling

10. Stop or No

IDEAS
INTO
PRACTICE

A

B

THANKS!!

DEVELOPING CULTURAL COMPETENCIES FOR WORK IN GLOBAL ENVIRONMENTS

SOUTH FLORIDA ODN

CAROL SUSAN DEVANEY, CPF, CPLP

Objectives

Participants will...

- Explore how their own cultural framework might affect their ability to work with others.

- Look at culture in its broadest sense.

- Visit the complexities of language and how it affects group communication.

- Exchange experiences and resources with each other.

Agenda

Exercise #1: Workplace Culture

Exercise #2: Fun with Language

Exercise #3: The Beauty of Diversity

Discussion and Idea Exchange

STAGES OF GROWTH
AWAY FROM ETHOCENTRISM

1. **Naïve/No Social Consciousness:**
    Basically this is when an individual is not even aware they are part of a group with specific values, norms, and ways of behaving.

2. **Acceptance:**
    This is when an individual is aware of a group's culture and buys into it.

3. **Resistance:**
    This happens when the premises of the individual's group are challenged. It is usually meet with what appears as a hostile, militant, or over-sensitive response.

4. **Redefinition:**
    This is when an individual is willing to question and look beyond the negative stereotypes his group may have had about other groups.

5. **Inclusion:**
    This is when the person looks for ways to communicate with others outside of his group.

Developing Cultural Competencies for Work in Global Environments

IDEAS INTO PRACTICE

THANKS!!

MINING THE GOLD:
A Diversity Initiative

Business Destination

Intent

Define diversity in the context of the business vision, anticipated market conditions, and desired culture.

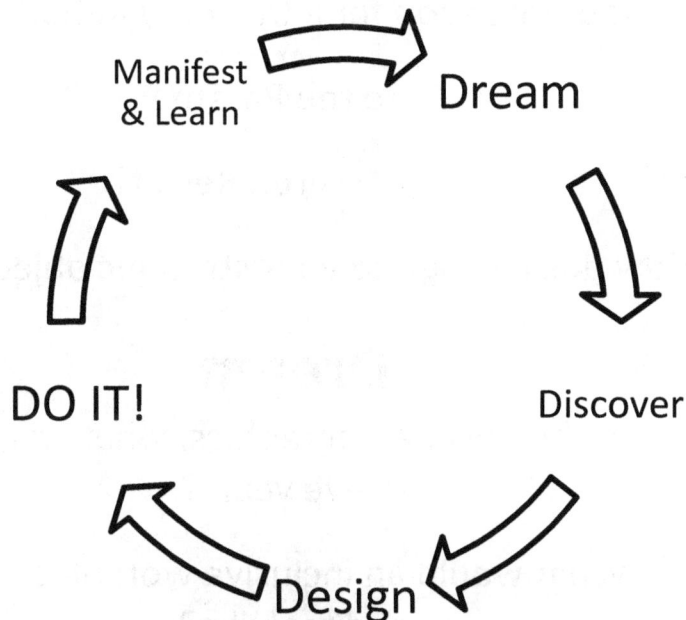

Manifest & Learn → Dream

Dream ↓ Discover

Design ↗ Discover

DO IT! ↑

DO IT! ↙ Design

Process for Developing an Inclusive Multicultural Workplace

Leadership Development

Current State

Process for Developing an Inclusive Multicultural Workplace

Intent

Given your business context and future   challenges, what is your intention for a Diversity Initiative?

What are the Parameters?

Desired Result?

How does it align to your strategic objectives?

Dream

Given the new demographics, what will be different in five years?

What would an inclusive workplace be and feel like?

What underlines exceptional leadership moments in terms of a diversity agenda?

What gives life to the organization?

Discover

Who is in your pipeline?

Do they represent a diversity of experiences,
cultures, and thinking?

How well do they work with people who think,
look, and behave differently from themselves?

Can they think on their feet?

Do they have the required skills to lead
in turbulent times?

Design

What changes in your customer processes need to be
made to attract and keep customers that represent the
new demographics?

How will we know when we have succeeded?

What internal support is needed?

Where are there interdependencies?

What innovations will bring the dream alive?

What are the implications of these changes
for internal staff?

DO IT!

Expand understanding of differences and
need for inclusion.

Elevate leaders' skills, expand their thinking,
and ability to collaborate.

Create an organization wide passion
for diversity.

Reengineer processes to delight your
multicultural customers.

Implement innovations.

Ongoing evaluation and feedback.

Manifest

Measure Results

Reflect

Celebrate Success
and Learning

A Brief Introduction to Crossing Cultures

facilitated by

Carol Susan DeVaney, CPF, CPLP
HR Florida Director of Diversity
DeVaney-Wong International

Objectives

Learn SHRM's definitions for Diversity and Inclusion

Have a basic understanding of elements that make up personal culture

Understand some fundamental steps needed to communicate across cultures

Leave with a resource list for further learning

Diversity...

the similarities and differences
between individuals accounting
for all aspects of one's personality
and individual identity.

Inclusion...

provides the potential for greater innovation and creativity. Inclusion is what enables organizations to realize the business benefits of this potential.

Diversity Discipline...

deals with the qualities, experiences and work styles that make individuals unique as well as how organizations can leverage those qualities in support of business objectives.

Culture
and
Ethocentrism

Awareness

Choices

Potential Change

Personal Culture

Geographic Culture

Workplace Culture

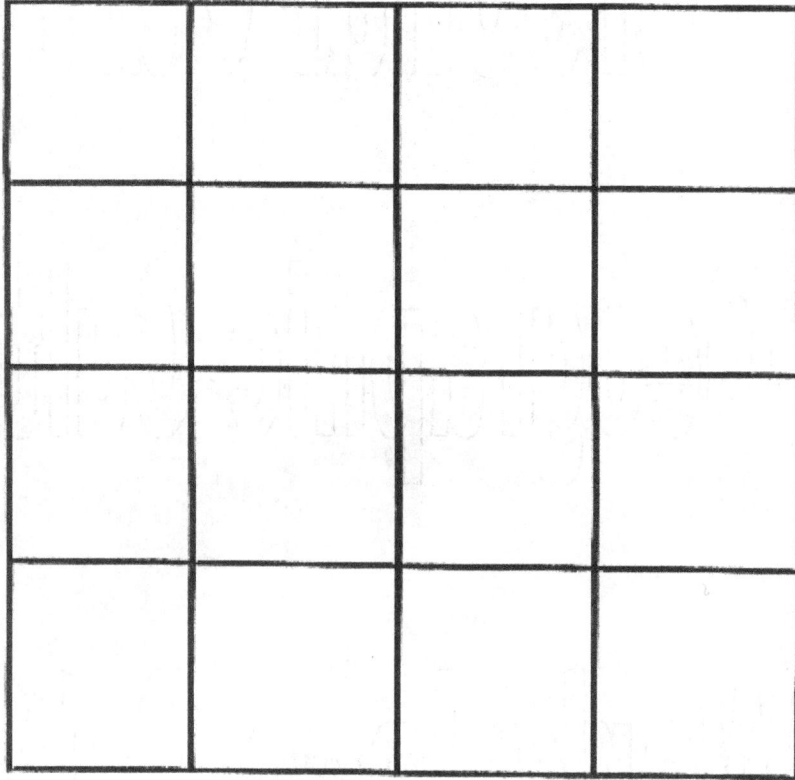

How many squares do you see?

#_____

Questions?

THANKS!!

The Art of Global
and
Cross Cultural
Competencies

July 2009

facilitated by
Carol Susan DeVaney, CPF, CPLP
DeVaney-Wong International

OBJECTIVES

Learn SHRM's definition for diversity

Begin to understand the hidden elements that make up culture

Explore your own cultural framework

Learn basic skills for cross cultural communication

Obtain a resource list for future action

DIVERSITY...
the similarities and differences between individuals accounting for all aspects of one's personality and individual identity.

INCLUSION...
provides the potential for greater innovation and creativity. Inclusion is what enables organizations to realize the business benefits of this potential.

GLOBAL COMPETENCIES...
skills needed to communicate and interact effectively in a global environment.

ETHNOCENTRISM

No awareness that one operates
within a specific cultural framework

⇩

Aware that their culture has rules
for operating

⇩

Aware that other cultures may not
share some values or ways
of doing things

⇩

Ability to see the positives and
potential negatives of both
cultural frameworks

AWARENESS

CHOICES

POTENTIAL CHANGE

PERSONAL CULTURE

With a partner describe to each other 2 or 3 things that have shaped who you are as a person.

SMALL FAMILY?   BIG FAMILY?

BIG CITY LIFE?   TRAVEL?

RURAL FARM FAMILY?

SIGNIFICANT MENTOR?

FAITH?

IMMIGRANT?

The focus of our work is to forge
a bridge between cultures of
divergent views, faiths, looks,
and all of the fantastic beauty of
diversity.

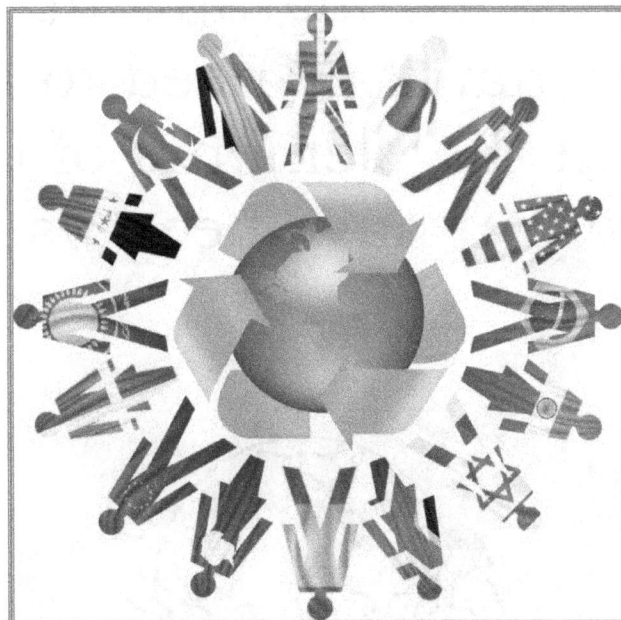

Geographic Culture

Tell the "immigrant" at your table what they need to know about the elements of U.S. Culture you have been assigned.

Workplace Culture

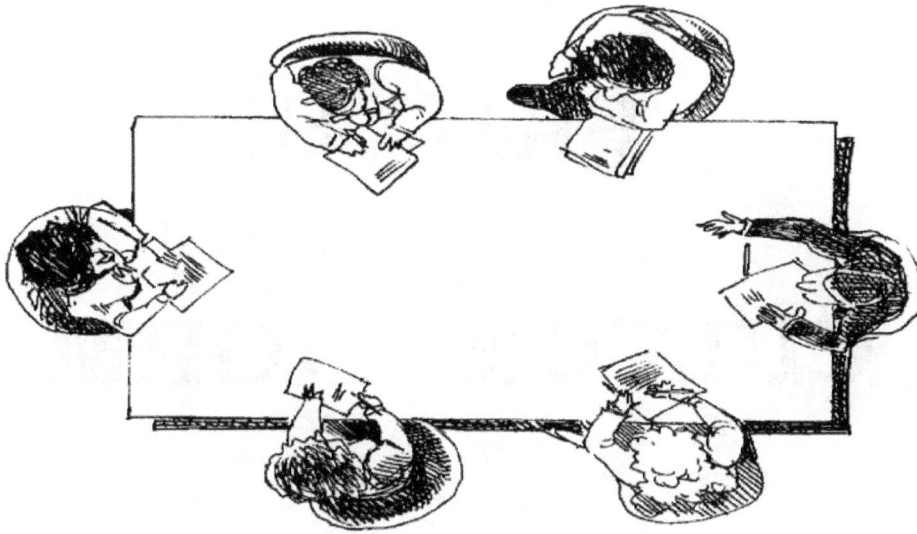

At minimum there is an interface of personal, geographic, and organizational cultures.

Let's look back at each of them.

ORGANIZATIONAL CULTURE

SKILLS

CULTURE NORM

360 SUPPORT

AGILITY

Diversity in Latin America

April 2008

Facilitated by
Carol Susan DeVaney, CPF, CPLP
DeVaney-Wong International, LLC

OBJECTIVES

Learn the fundamentals of
ethnocentrism

Understand how creating a
diverse workforce requires
fundamental organizational
change

Practice a sample experience
in Appreciative Inquiry

Have fun!

Stages
of
Growth
Away
From

ETHNOCENTRISM

Stage 1

NAÏVE
NO SOCIAL
CONSCIOUSNESS

Basically this is when an individual is not even aware that they are part of a group with specific values, norms, and ways of behaving.

Stage 2

ACCCPTANCE

Here the individual is aware of the group's "culture" and agrees to be part of it.

Stage 3

RESISTANCE

This is when members of a group are questioned or challenged about the premises of their group. Usually this is met with what appears as a hostile, militant, or over-sensitive response.

Stage 4

REDEFINITION

This is when individuals are willing to question their group norms and values and look beyond the negative stereotypes they may have about other groups.

diversity

Stage 5

BUILDING BRIDGES

This is when the person looks for ways to communicate with others outside his group.

"Start with what you have in common."

A Culture of Inclusion

An Organizational Change Model

Nothing changes unless the forces pushing for change are stronger than the forces resisting change.

People and organizations change because of

PAIN

OR

GAIN

There are three levels
at which
organizations change

Knowledge

Attitude

Cultural

What Does

Inclusion Feel Like?

Your Current
Organizational
Culture
and
Inclusion…?

Problem solving
consists of naming a
problem, figuring out
what is causing it and
then

FIX IT

Appreciative inquiry looks for what works and describes what it would look like if those strengths are highlighted or tapped.

Discovery

Dream

Affirmative Topic

Destiny

Design

4-D's

Dr. David L. Cooperider

?

What
is your
provocative
proposition?

How to be a Diversity Chair

2009 HR Florida State Council

Carol Susan DeVaney, CPF, CPLP
HR Florida Diversity Director

converted from a powerpoint presentation

- 2007 the SHRM Board approved a revitalized five year strategy/vision for the Diversity and Inclusion Initiative

"Be a leading resource and provider of workplace diversity through leadership, strategies, competitive business practices, and professional development for HR professionals and business leaders."

SHRM 2008's Three Major Efforts

1. **Leadership Summit on Diversity – a 56 page executive summary available on website**

2. **International Diversity Research – joint work with Economist Intelligence Unit- global survey and in-depth interviews which resulted in**

    - DRI – Diversity Readiness Index that assesses the diversity environment in leading industrial and developing countries
    - D-MAT – an online assessment tool executives can take to compare their attitudes to those of peer

3. **Conducted a comprehensive Diversity Content/Practice Analysis in cooperation with the folk who do PHR, SPHR, etc**

Exploring a Certificate and possibly a Certification Process for D&I practitioners.

SHRM's Proposed 2009 Goals

1. Host a second Leadership Summit on Diversity and Inclusion

2. Publish the results of the International Diversity Research

3. Begin implementation of short and long-term recommendations from Diversity Practice Analysis

4. Design and launch at least three new diversity products to members and non-members including the SHRM Diversity and Inclusion Certificate Program

SHRM Diversity Resources

www.shrm.org
click Diversity Core Leadership area
and also look at Volunteer Resources

Other resources
1. Tool Kits
2. Web casts
3. Power point presentations
4. Articles
5. Diversity Newsletter
6. Diversity Q&A Section
7. Publications
8. Conference Calls
9. SHRM Diversity Conference
10. Our Florida Resources

Three Challenges from SHRM's Ten Strategies for Achieving a More Diverse Membership

1. **Failing to make the value of SHRM membership clear to potential members.**
    Why would they want to join?
    What value does SHRM and your Chapter have to offer them?

2. **Failing to be sensitive to potential feelings of social and professional discomfort.**
    What is the culture of your Chapter?

3. **Creating an environment or perception that discourages participation.**
    Is there an "in group" and an "out group"?
    Do members know how they can contribute?

An exercise in understanding your Chapter's Culture

o Describe your Chapter's culture to your partner.

o What are the three most important things a potential member should know about how to become a productive member of your SHRM Chapter?

o On a scale of 1 to 7 with 7 being "completely welcoming and participatory for members" and 1 being "seen as cliquish and unwelcoming to newcomers" where does your Chapter's Culture stand? How can you move it up a notch?

Thank You!

LEADERSHIP

LEADERSHIP

Effective Communication
&
Crucial Discussions for Leadership

June 16, 2009

facilitated by

Carol Susan DeVaney, CPF, CPLP
DeVaney Wong International, LLC

249

For Your Notes...

Agenda

Morning

1. Introductions

2. Objectives and Participant Expectations

3. Fundamentals of Communication

4. Test Your Listening Skills

5. Elements of an Effective Message – A Communication Model

6. Persuasion

7. Trust – Key Ingredient

8. Elements of "Culture" in Communication

(Lunch Break)

Afternoon

9. Preparing for Potentially Difficult Communication

10. Assessing Your Conflict Style

11. Fundamentals for Positive Conflict Management

12. Practice

13. Closing and Evaluation

Objectives

Participants will...

✓ learn a model for effective communication

✓ evaluate their listening skills

✓ understand how trust affects communication

✓ improve their ability to engage in important communication

✓ discover their conflict style

✓ explore ways to prevent and resolve conflict

✓ practice realistic scenarios

Communication Model

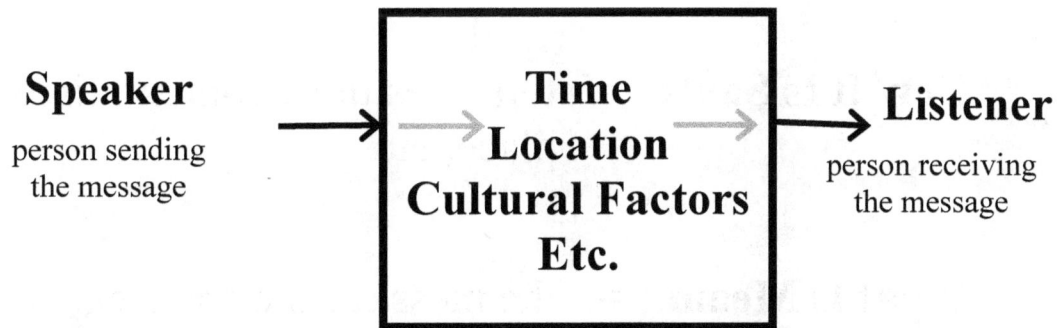

Speaker	Time	Listener
person sending the message	Location	person receiving the message
	Cultural Factors	
	Etc.	

Spoken words account for 30-35% of the meaning of a message.

Three Parts of the Message

What Is Said   =   the actual words

How It Is Said   =   tone, gestures, context, time, place, etc.

What Is Meant   =   the message the speaker attempts to deliver

Listening Skills

High levels of "emotional intelligence" are correlated with good listening skills.

From a list of items, people can remember about 7. With last words of unrelated sentences the average is 2.8 items.

People can recall about 17% of the content of the evening news. If prompted they can recall about 25%.

A person can talk at a rate of 125-175 words per minute. We can listen at up to 450 words per minute.

30-35% of how we understand a message is the spoken word.

In business and academic settings listening is in the top 3 skills noted for successful leaders

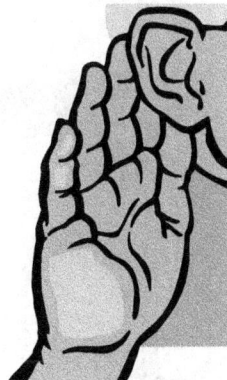

Listening Preference

PEOPLE FOCUSED =
These folks tend to be deeply concerned about how others feel. May be seen as intrusive and over involved.

ACTION FOCUSED =
These folks want to get to the bottom line quickly and want others to be organized and brief. They tend to try to finish the speaker's thoughts and can be seen as blunt.

CONTENT FOCUSED =
Likes people to back up their statements with research or facts. Keeps wanting more and more detail before making decisions.

TIME FOCUSED =
These folks tend to tell you how much time they can allot you and tend to interrupt and rush people.

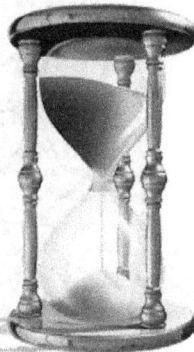

Listening Strategies

"**Affirmative listening**" tries to silence our internal critic by trying to hear everything and seeking out new ideas, common ground, and shared beliefs and looking at it as an opportunity to learn more about the person and the situation.

Sometimes if you suspect there will be resistance to hearing what you have to say, you can acknowledge this out loud, like: "I know what I am going to say may sound unreasonable, but can you help me out by hearing it all the way through?" This is called "Couching."

Questions To Ask Yourself

?   Was I listening affirmatively?

?   Did I clarify that I understand what you meant?

?   What am I supposed to do with this information?

Four Reasons People Communicate

To Persuade Someone

↑

To Provide Information

↑

To Express Their Feelings

↑

To Establish Contact

Team Work & Trust Video

As you view the video job down key advice
the peer coach gives our main character.

TRANSLATION

Directions: In your small group try to translate the following statement into the language you have been assigned.

Í need you stop touching that piece of equipment when you are not wearing gloves."

Translation…

Teaching People Skills in "Crucial Confrontations" has resulted in...

- 40% ↑ in productivity

- 30% ↑ in quality

- 50% ↓ in costs

- 20% ↑ in employee satisfaction

—from Vital Smarts research

Conflict Styles

1) **Avoiding**

2) **Smoothing**

3) **Forcing**

4) **Bargaining**

5) **Problem Solving**

The Conflict Radar at Work

Sometimes we are so busy or distracted that we find ourselves surprised or blindsided into a conflict situation. The following are strategies that will help you identify potential conflict early to prevent and/or resolve it.

1) **Think Ahead** — As you go about your daily business think about the Who, What, When, How, Why or Where of potential conflict.

2) **Ask for Information** — Find out how others are feeling or what they are thinking about issues, situations or people. Don't assume you know.

3) **Inform** — Let others know how you think or feel in open but non-threatening ways.

4) **Future Focused** — Try to keep the conversation moving towards the future. In other words: What could be possible? What would success look like? What is the person's interest, not position?

Setting the Stage

Think Before You Speak!

? | Are you confronting about
the right problem or
issue?

? | Are you ready to
discuss the issue
with the other
person as a
person and not as
the enemy?

How do you know if you have the right problem?

?   Do the solutions you get achieve the results you want?

?   Do you find yourself constantly going back to discuss the same problem?

?   Do you find yourself getting more worked up than the "problem" should be causing?

Three Levels of a Problem

Level **1**

The first time it happens you may just want to describe it.

Level **2**

The next time it happens you need to describe the fact that this may be a pattern of behavior.

Level **3**

If the problem continues to reoccur, you need to discuss how it affects the relationship.

And the Problem Is?

Your teenage daughter got her driver's license last week. She drives herself and her two best friends to her first big dance 20 minutes away. You have discussed your concerns and she agreed to come home by 11 p.m. and take her cell phone in case of an emergency. She is now an hour late, and when you try to call her cell phone, it rings in her bedroom where she left it. She comes in 1¼ hours late.

1) What is the problem?

2) Describe it in one sentence.

C   =
Content

P   =
Pattern

R   =
Relationship

Adapted from <u>Crucial Confrontations</u>

Problems typically are not the
behavior, but the actual
consequences of the behavior.

Other times the problem is not
about the behavior or the
consequences but about the
person's original intentions.

So what is it that you want or
don't want for you, the other
person, and for the relationship?

Be careful: Silence may not make
the problem go away.

Keep Focused on the Future

Basically conversations occur in...

Past   What got us here / History

Present   What is happening or what is about to happen

Future   What you would like to imagine happening

Some Tips for Future Focus

1) The **past** establishes a connection to the future, but it s historical, so it involves what worked or did not work then. It does not address the present or the future.

    "We tried that before and it did not work."

2) **Present** conversation involved what is currently happening or what is about to happen. It involves current action.

    "When our meeting ends today, I will call and get some pricing."

3) **Future**-focused conversation is a conversation that focuses on possibilities or potential.

    "What if we could figure out a way to speed production without compromising safety?"

The Request — A Tool of Persuasion

Usually people will only change what they are doing if they see what is in it for them: **pain** or **gain**.

A **request** is a change-focused conversation. It has three parts:

1) **What** do you want done

2) **When** does it need to be done

3) **Who** is going to do it

New Order:

PAST → FUTURE → PRESENT

Unfair Communication Techniques

1) **Pretending that the other person has made an unreasonable statement or demand.**
   "You make such a big deal out of nothing!"

2) **Jumping to conclusions or "mind reading."**
   "Don't even try. I know what you want."

3) **Switching the subject.**
   "That reminds me, do you remember what we talked about last week...?

4) **Bringing up more than one accusation at a time.**
   "Not only are you inconsiderate but you're lazy too!"

5) **Bragging or keeping score.**
   "You don't try as hard as I do."

6) **Being logical when someone is talking about their feelings.**
   "Don't be so dramatic. You'll get another job.

7) **Interrupting.**
   "Excuse me but. . . ."

8) **Intimidating, yelling, or exploding.**
   "You *(censored)* of a *(censored)*!"

9) **Denying the other person's experience.**
   "You shouldn't feel like that."

10) **Using <u>You</u> rather that <u>I</u> statements.**
    "You really make me angry!"

What Can You Do?

Too Rigid?

Tom is new on your team. He is a hard worker but tends to see things as right or wrong and seems to not have any flexibility. He also tends to do "what if" to the point where you can't seem to finish any project. He came from an academic research center and you are afraid he is not adjusting. You are a peer and prefer not to go to his boss, but you are getting ready to miss a second key deadline due to his pickiness.

We Always Do It Like This

You were hired to bring creative ideas to the team because your prior employer was known as a positive maverick in the field of water conservation. However, every time you make a suggestion you are told why it will not work here. There is a severe dranput and you have some non-traditional ideas that worked in your last job.

How can you approach the team?

These Are The Results

A very influential person comes to you about the results of your research and suggests your scenarios seem too alarmist to them. The fact is you have done the numbers and checked it out with some valued colleagues and feel you are providing realistic situations. This person wants you to "soften" your wording. You do not report to them but they are very high ranking.

What can you do?

Always Something

Tanya is liked by everyone, but she is turning out to be unreliable. She doesn't meet the deadlines the groups set and always has an excuse. You know she has family issues, but she volunteered to be on this committee. Others covered for her, but resentment is building. You are the team leader.

What do you do?

Embarrassing

You go out with Bill on a field visit. At lunch in a public restaurant you run into some contractors who see your badge and make some smart aleck remark about how they will never get work from your office because "they don't have friends in high places." Bill is not in a good mood and snaps back with a nasty comment.

What can you do?

Suggested Readings

The Emotional Intelligence Quick Book.
   Travis Bradberry and Jean Greaves.
   Simon & Schuster, 2005.

Multicultural Manners. Norine Dresser.
   John Wiley, 2005

Are You Really Listening? Paul J.
   Donoghue and Mary E. Siegel, Ave
   Maria Press, 2005.

Crucial Conversations. Kerry Patterson,
   Joseph Grenny, Ron McMillan and Al
   Switzer. McGraw Hill, 2002.

Crucial Confrontations. Kerry Patterson,
   Joseph Grenny, Ron McMillan and Al
   Switzer. McGraw Hill, 2005.

STRATEGICALLY LEADING CHANGE

Presented by

Carol Susan DeVaney, CPF, SPLP
DeVaney-Wong International, LLC

For Your Notes

OBJECTIVES

Participants will...

❖ Learn what works and what doesn't in executing a change process

❖ Understand individual reactions to change and how to effectively deal with them

❖ Be able to identify typical organizational phases of change and how they relate to an organization's life cycle

❖ Work with a model for facilitating organizational change

❖ Explore case examples from the facilitator and other participants

❖ Understand what role they as leaders or HR practitioners can effectively play

❖ Obtain helpful resources to utilize back in the office immediately

AGENDA

Day #1

Introductions

- ➢ What Motivates Change
- ➢ Understanding How Individuals Respond to Change
- ➢ Elements of Successful Change
- ➢ Common Change Pitfalls

Day #2

- ➢ Phases in Organizational Transition
- ➢ Levels of Desired Change
- ➢ Strategic Models for Change
- ➢ Ideas Into Practice
- ➢ Action Plan and Evaluation

Pain or Gain

There are only two reasons why organizations or individuals undergo a change process

Current or Anticipated **PAIN**

Current or Anticipated **GAIN**

So a fundamental question you must ask yourself about every member of your team is "why would they want to do things differently?"

Common Reactions Individuals Have to Change

1. **People will feel awkward, ill at ease and self-conscious.**

   Like being a fish in a bowl.

2. **People will be concerned about what they have to give up -- loss.**

   It is unlikely they will first think of what might be gained.

3. **People will be concerned they don't have enough time, money or resources.**

   Perhaps more critical they fear loosing their status as experts and being in a learner role.

4. **People can handle only so much change at a time.**

5. **People are ready for and react to change differently. Some jump in and soon run out of steam, while others gradually increase momentum.**

6. **People will feel alone even if everyone else is going through the change.**

7. **As soon as the pressure is off, there is a tendency to want things to go back to how they were.**

DON'T LET CHANGE
KNOCK YOU OFF YOUR FEET

Tip Sheet for Coping with Change

1. Give yourself permission to be in a learning posture. We all need time to understand and adjust to change.

2. Keep a check on your anticipatory anxiety. Often the anticipation of the unknown is more stressful than the actual event.

3. Focus on what you want not on what you fear.

4. Sort out what you can and can't control. Try to keep yourself in a position where you can make some of the choices even if they are small ones.

5. Get help. Others may not realize you need help, or they may not know what kind of help you need.

6. Don't compare yourself to others who are going through similar situations. They can be a great source of support, but everyone does not react the same to risk and ambiguity.

7. Take time out to recharge. Sometimes we get so involved in the change process we lose total perspective on the situation.

8. It is a struggle to leave the old behind, but in doing so, we face new experiences and opportunities.

9. Give yourself credit. You did not get to the age you are without having some success at managing change. Review those successes and make them work for you.

10. Give others credit. Success tends to generate success.

Breaking Old Assumptions

in the Workplace

Loyalty & Security

Traditional: LOYALTY assumes a reciprocal dependent relationship. I, the worker, am loyal to you and you in turn will take care of me = SECURITY

Seniority & Continuous Learning

The assumption that seniority gave us a special edge is being challenged since skills are becoming obsolete in much shorter increments.

The worker who is keeping up not only with current but also with emerging technologies is now prized. This worker may not have as much "experience" or age.

For the first time in our history we have four distinct generations in the workplace.

Hierarchy vs Flatness

The supervisor/employee ratio makes leading by position very difficult. Employees need to make decisions at lower levels to be responsive to time and customer pressures.

Incremental vs Constant Change

Customer demands, global competition, and constantly changing technology do not always allow the luxury of incremental change.

Those who can see constant turmoil as the way business will be done, not as a temporary phenomenon, will survive. Agility is seen as key to survival.

PARADIGMS

1. What are some of the negative paradigms that exist about your organization or your industry?

2. What are some paradigms that negatively affect my department? My team?

3. What are some paradigms I am operating under that may not be effective?

4. What can I do to challenge assumptions?

ORGANIZATIONAL REACTIONS TO CHANGE

DENIAL/DISBELIEF

People act as if nothing is happening. There is a general numbness. There is apathy and a sense of "this too will pass." Disbelief that "they really mean" the change. Focus is on the past and you see lots of activity but little end result or a shutting down.

The most important task for the manager is to confront the individuals with truthful information. Let them know the change will happen, what is expected from them and how they can prepare themselves.

Worst thing to do: Bring in a motivational speaker or celebrate.

HECK NO/SADNESS

Here you see anger, disappointment and opposition. Groups round up the wagons; lack of cooperation. There is a sense of generalized negativity. Here you may see accidents, absenteeism, illnesses and general acting out.

The most important task for the manager is to allow the feelings to emerge and to manage the conflict. People who had been competently self assured may be unsettled.

Worst thing to do: Not allow people the opportunity to express apprehensions, fears, concerns.

LEARNING CURVE

People begin to try new things. As a manager this can be an overwhelming time because people deluge you with new ideas and suggestions and you might even feel like your authority is challenged. The group feels like there is too much to do and not a clear focus or direction. You see people slowly beginning to accept the change but many are anxious about the new skills they must learn.

The task for the manager here is to help set goals, help prioritize and help facilitate problem solving.

Worst thing to do: Not allow for mistakes. We are never experts at something new. Reward steps in the right direction. Don't wait for complete success to reward. Recognize that formal training may be needed.

THE WAY IT IS

People begin to see the change as "the way it is." They begin to actively participate and contribute to the change. You see people initiating their work again and individuals begin to become teams again.

The task of the manager is to facilitate "team building." Folks are settling into new roles and ways of doing things and old team patterns and norms may not apply.

Worst thing to do: Slack off and assume it is finished. Do not be surprised when people slide back. It is important that you keep consistently focused on where you want to go.

ORGANIZATIONAL CLIMATE

Think about the current assessment climate in the organization you are trying to help change. Check characteristics which apply.

	1.	People avoid taking risks
	2.	People are cynical
	3.	Nobody wants to own up to any problems
	4.	Mistakes are seen as a necessary part of learning
	5.	There is a sense that how well you perform matters
	6.	People are rigid about rules and policies
	7.	Accountability is low
	8.	Not making mistakes is valued more than how well you perform
	9.	Everyone feels they are under attack
	10.	People feel that they are valued by the team
	11.	The atmosphere seems chaotically busy but not necessarily productive
	12.	New ideas and disagreements are accepted

Organizational Climate Scoring:

Put a check mark next to the statement numbers from the assessment.

Entitlement Atmosphere

_____1

_____6

_____7

_____8   Total _____

High Threat Atmosphere

_____2

_____3

_____9

_____11   Total _____

Performance Based Atmosphere

_____4

_____5

_____10

_____12   Total _____

ORGANIZATIONAL CLIMATE SNAPSHOTS

Entitlement

People avoid taking risks by focusing and adhering to strict rules and policies…lots of red tape. The focus is on not making mistakes rather than performance. There is very little accountability because the focus is on the rule checking, not the outcome.

High Threat

People feel cynical and vulnerable. Trust is low. There is a fear of exposing any problems and people are quick to point fingers when they emerge. There is a lot of stress and chaos but often little to show for it. Everyone is focused on saving themselves and building their little empire.

PERFORMANCE BASED

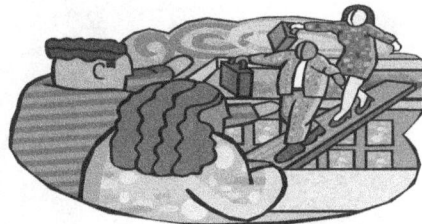

It is clear about its vision and innovation and trying out new things is rewarded. Mistakes are seen as necessary to learning but there are clear accountability expectations. A sense of team is supported because the group's outcomes are rewarded. Change is easier to implement in a performance based climate. What can leaders do to address the challenges in an entitled or a highly fearful environment?

```
┌─────────────────────────┐
│                         │
│  ENTITLEMENT            │
│        ┌────────────────┴──────────┐
│        │                           │
└────────┤  HIGH THREAT              │
         │              ┌────────────┴──────────────────┐
         │              │                               │
         └──────────────┤  PERFORMANCE                  │
                        │  BASED                        │
                        │                               │
                        └───────────────────────────────┘
```

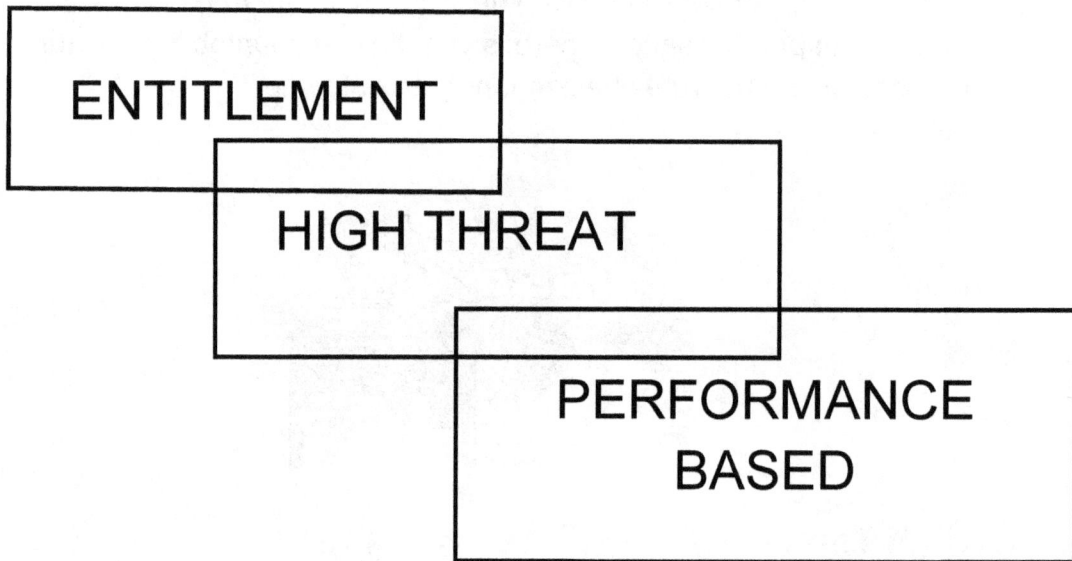

Trust is a key element in a performance based environment.
How can each of us continue to build trust?

KEY INGREDIENTS FOR
ORGANIZATIONAL SURVIVAL/SUCCESS

SKILL	This is like wearing shoes when you go to work. You must have the technical and people skills required for the job and must always be involved in continuous learning.
CULTURE	You must know not only what your job is but how it fits with what is valued and rewarded in the organization. What are the unspoken do's and taboos?
A 360° HELPING HAND	The old adage should really say, "It is WHAT you know and WHO you know." It is critical to have a mentor who can give you a hand up, a network to keep you informed and a support system to help you feel engaged.
AGILITY	With the rapid changes in today's workplace, the capacity for flexibility and creativity are a must. Managing change successfully is a survival strategy.

ASSESSING YOUR STRENGTHS/VULNERABILITY

1. How has the current organizational climate impacted you and your department?

2. What are you currently doing to keep ahead of new advances and expectations?

3. Who are your mentors? Are they appropriate choices?

4. What shape is your network in?

5. What helps you cope with constant change?

ISSUES THAT GET IN THE WAY
OF SUCCESSFUL CHANGE

Look at these 8 barriers to successful change. Which have you seen in action?

1. **The Desired End is Not Clear**

   People do not understand where the organization wants to end up. People do not understand the why of the change.

2. **Lack of Conviction in the Change**

   Key people do not believe the change will be positive in the long run. In the past there has been lots of rhetoric about change but nothing has happened, or change has been poorly implemented in the past.

3. **Pretending Nobody Will Oppose the Change**

   Resistance is a natural response to change. Even if people want the change, they will not like the uncertainty or disruption it causes. This is particularly dangerous with middle managers because they have to lead the process.

4. **Failure to Communicate Clearly**

   This is the time to manage and direct communication as clearly as possible.

5. **Not Rewarding the Right Things**

   People will not take new ways of doing things seriously unless they understand how they will benefit from adapting or how they will suffer for not doing so.

6. **Lack of Tolerance for Errors**

   If an organization has historically rewarded low risk-taking by punishing mistakes and not rewarding innovation, this will be a hard paradigm shift.

7. **Lack of Orchestration**

   It is important to see the whole picture and seeing how the different pieces will fit together. Remember the "white space."

8. **Lack of Persistence**

   Large-scale organizational change requires a lengthy time commitment and constant readjustment and re-evaluation.

KEYS TO MAKING ORGANIZATIONAL CHANGE WORK

Instructions: The following are key elements to helping organizations succeed in change. On a scale of 1 to 7 with 1 being poor and 7 being excellent, how well are you attending to these elements?

_____1. We have good reason to do it.

_____2. Person(s) leading the change are respected and valued by those that have to be a part of the change.

_____3. The key folks in the change process have been included in planning and execution design.

_____4. We are creating cross-functional groups that can anticipate and work out problems that will emerge.

_____5. We are coaching and training people on the skills and attitudes that will be needed.

_____6 We have pictured the change through new logos, new words, new traditions, and other visible means at the right time in the process.

_____7. We acknowledge resistance and confusion as normal. It is unlikely everyone will be on board at the same time.

_____8. We have celebrated steps in the right direction and hitting early wins.

_____9. We have used outside help, when needed, to clarify our vision, keep us focused, and reinforce our position.

_____10. We recognize that in today's environment we are looking at continuous change. We reward flexibility, adaptation, and agility rather than loyalty, seniority, and not making waves.

PHASES IN AN ORGANIZATION'S LIFE CYCLE

Start Up
Few people, long hours. Rules being made up as needed. Salaries usually not good. Lots of unknowns but room for creativity.

Rapid Growth
Rapid growth and customer demands. Loose structure and people take on multiple roles. Much uncertainty. Thin line between success and chaos. Constant need for more/different resources.

Structure
Growth begins to stabilize and formal structure gets put in place to manage it. Employees begin to have some longevity and the organization has a clear sense of history.

Maturation
Distinct established culture. Lots of structure and procedures. Implementing change is more difficult because boundaries are more rigid.   What has made them successful in the past can hurt their future.

Change can be needed at

ANY or ALL

of the phases

LEVELS OF CHANGE

COSMETIC

This is when you make minor, incremental, cosmetic or simply accommodating changes.

Example
This can be a new logo or marketing focus.

STRUCTURAL

This is when change involves the whole organization. It involves developing new ways of operating.

Example
Going from one to 3 locations.

TRANSFORMATIONAL

Most radical of all change. It is breaking the paradigm. It is sudden and extensive. It redefines what you do and who you are as an organization.

Example
Electric lines vs a new power grid system.

PARADIGMS

1. What are some of the paradigms we are operating under in our organization?

2. What organization would we want to be compared to positively?

3. What is the worst future scenario for our organization?

4. My "ideal" for our organization would be that...

5. My contribution to that ideal would be...

COMMON REASONS FOR CHANGE

CUSTOMER	Customers are not accepting what and how we give them goods and services. With mass media, they have raised their level of awareness and standards for consumption.
COMPETITION	Our competition can often come from unexpected sources.
INNOVATION	New discoveries or new cultural frameworks can make old ways obsolete.
GLOBAL ECONOMY	What happens "THERE" affects us "HERE". What are some other factors that are affecting you?
CHANGE	Change is pervasive and consistent. Change is not something with a beginning or an end. It is a constant.

From a systems standpoint, no matter what the change is,

it will have an effect on the

WHOLE!

FORCE FIELD ANALYSIS

Forces Pushing   **Forces Resisting**

Status Quo

(Remaining the Same)

Think of an action or change you want to make. Describe the forces supporting your decision and the forces resisting. What can you do to either increase the support or decrease the resistance?

KEY ROLES IN CHANGE

1. **Sponsors**   Those who have the power to
                   ???? positions or resources to
                   legitimize a change.

2. **Advocates**   These are people who advocate the
                   change but do not have the power in
                   the organization to sponsor it.

3. **Agents**   The people who actually make the
                   change happen, carry it out.

4. **Targets**   The people who will be impacted.

5. **Challengers** Those brave enough to ask questions
                    and disagree.

ROLES IN CHANGE

❖ You can be all of these at one time or another

❖ In your organization's current situation, what role can you play? Why?

❖ Think of a current change you want to make. Whose name can you put next to each category?

Sponsor   _____

Advocate   _____

Agent   _____

Target   _____

Challenger   _____

STEPS IN CHANGE EXECUTION

The following are 6 questions that can help shape the process for executing the change.

Question # 1
"What is the compelling reason why this change has to happen now?"

Question # 2
"What will success look like if we accomplish it?"

Question # 3
"Who do I need supporting the change and what will their roles be?"

Question # 4
"What is the most effective way to proceed that takes the potential risk that may come with the change into consideration?"

Question # 5
"What do we need to do to make sure we are on the right track towards meeting our goals?"

When you reach your destination it is important to ask one closing question:

Question #6
"Did we succeed as expected and what lessons did we learn for future efforts?"

Question # 1
"What is the compelling reason why this change has to happen now?"

What tasks would you expect to have as a change facilitator during this phase?

What tasks would you expect a leader to have?

"What will success look like if we accomplish it?"

What tasks would you expect to have as a change
facilitator during this phase?

What tasks would you expect a leader to have?

Question # 3

"Who do I need supporting the change and what will their roles be?"

What tasks would you expect to have as a change facilitator during this phase?

What tasks would you expect a leader to have?

Question # 4

"What is the most effective way to proceed that takes the potential risk that may come with the change into consideration?"

What tasks would you expect to have as a change facilitator during this phase?

What tasks would you expect a leader to have?

"What do we need to do to make sure we are on the right track towards meeting our goals?"

What tasks would you expect to have as a change facilitator during this phase?

What tasks would you expect a leader to have?

Question # 6
"Did we succeed as expected and what lessons did we learn for future efforts?"

What tasks would you expect to have as a change facilitator during this phase?

What tasks would you expect a leader to have?

CHALLENGES TO STRATEGIC PLANNING
AND MEASURING SUCCESS

1.	A mission statement with elements so broad and general it does not really differentiate your organization from any other one.
2.	General goals and objectives focus more on the how and less on the desired outcome.
3.	Affected stakeholders are not solicited for input.
4.	Goals and strategies are formulated with evaluation measures in mind.
5.	Identifying strategies for achieving the goals which are actually just brainstorming or "laundry lists."
6.	Weak linkage between strategic goals, performance measures and resources available.
7.	Inadequate discussion of external factors that can be impacting the process.
8.	Leadership challenges or conflicts that are not attended to.
9.	Lack of insight into how one system might impact another.
10.	Not enough thought to how quickly the data will provide insight into how successful the process is going and/or whether you even have the capacity to generate and evaluate the data.

FROM THE EMPLOYEE'S POINT OF VIEW

Think of a change process you have recently been a part of or witnessed and answer the following questions.

1.   How did the leadership describe the reason for the change?

2. What was done to clarify what the desired results would be?

3. Was the plan to get from point A to point B clear to everyone?

4. Do you think every employee in the organization understood his/her role in making the change happen?

Now go back and describe the leadership behaviors that did or did not make it succeed.

SELLING CHANGE

For you to sell a massive change process, you must have answers to the following questions:

1. Why do we exist at all?

2. What changes are occurring in the nation and locally that are pushing us to change?

3. What is changing in the customers I serve? (How are people perceiving my service or product differently? How is my customer being redefined?)

4. What are the current problems we are having as an organization? (too much red tape, too little authority at a line level, outdated services, financial shortfalls, poor leadership, etc.

5. Why won't waiting or small incremental changes do the trick?

6. What will happen if we do not change?

7. What do we want to look like at the end of the change?

The answers to these questions give you your justification or "case" for change.

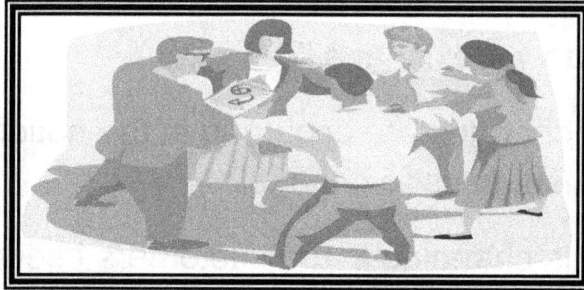

SAMPLE SITUATIONS

Bad Energy

SCENARIO #1

Jason has always been somewhat negative, but the team puts up with his whining because basically he is a hard worker and has a good heart. Since the V.P. announced some of the changes that will be happening, he has been difficult to be around – so much that when he is not in the office, the mood is considerably more positive. People keep trying to avoid him at all costs, and it is beginning to affect team communication.

Apparently your boss, Tonya, had a chat with him today, because when you got back from the warehouse, he cornered you and started ranting about how Tonya wants him to "pretend everything is just perfect."

How do you respond? As a team member but not a "boss," what can you do to help?

Not Listening

SCENARIO #2

Maria is a peer and the new supervisor to her team. She came from another division in Arizona and has a lot of ideas of how "things can be improved." She is bright, and you know she means well, but she is irritating her whole team, and from what you hear from your other peers they too are fed up with the "back in Arizona…" thing.

You work well together and one day both of you are alone in the office early. She catches you off guard and asks you, "What am I doing wrong? I am trying hard to make some much needed changes here. That is why I was hired. I like the people and think this group can reach the same level of production my old group had. You have been around for a long time and people trust you. Any suggestions?"

What do you respond? Is this an appropriate question? How can you be helpful?

Waste of Time

SCENARIO #3

Clyde is on a committee with you designed to make some recommendations to management regarding ways to cut costs. You have no idea why he volunteered for the committee because he shows up late, doesn't complete his assignments, and just in general doesn't seem to take it seriously.

Several people in the group have asked you to talk to him since the two of you have known each other for a while.

Another team member tried to approach him publicly last week, and he said, "Who do they think they are kidding? This committee is a waste of time and just a way for management to tell the big shots they had staff input." You do not agree with him.

How would you approach this?

The Rumors

SCENARIO #4

Every time there is an article in the paper about your company, John goes into crazy speculations regarding lay-offs, outsourcing, and other catastrophic scenarios. He feeds the rumors. Both of you are supervisors and you find the whole thing upsetting. There is enough real stuff going on without the rumors and catastrophizing John stirs up.

How do rumors affect a change effort?

As a peer what can you do?

What Is Mine Is Mine

SCENARIO #5

You supervise Marta and Sal. Marta and Sal had always cooperated well with one another, and when one team got in a pinch, the other would help out. Since Tod, the CEO, announced there may be some reductions in your department, you notice Sal has been much less friendly and, several times in meetings when Marta has asked for help, has told her his folks are too busy. Now Marta is turning him down for help. Both have worked well for over ten years and are good people. It is creating bad feelings all around and a couple of times has made whole department look bad.

What can you do?

The Dinosaur

SCENARIO #6

You have been in the department for about 6 months. You are fairly new at management, but the reason you were hired is you have a strong technology background and this department is in need of an update in its equipment and processes.

Jack has been with the department over 25 years and from his past evaluations you can tell he was a high performer and was responsible for several innovations ten years ago. You thought he would be a great help as you implemented these changes, but every time you approach him to serve on a committee or get some training, he tells you he will be retiring soon. You discover that, because of his wife's health problems and his age, it will be unlikely that he would retire any sooner than 5 years from now. You simply cannot wait that long.

What would you do?

We Already Tried That

SCENARIO #7

You are promoted to senior management. The person before you, Sonia, had been hired from the "outside" to make major changes. She was here for over two months and you know she made a lot of change efforts but things always seemed to fall flat before anything was completed.

Folks seemed to be happy about your promotion, but now as you try to make changes the staff laughs and tells you you should know better as it obviously did not work for Sonia. They seem to think that now that you are in charge everything can just go back to the way things were. The fact is the department must make changes.

What can you say to the team?

Bad Idea

SCENARIO #8

The County is thinking of implementing new software in your department. Your boss is quite excited about it and tells you he expects you to manage a smooth implementation.

As you study the materials, you realize this is just not going to meet the needs of the citizens that use your services. When you approach him about this, he accuses you of not being a team player and trying to find an excuse to get out of work. You are quite offended by his attitude but know he is under a lot of pressure to do this as this is a pet project of the new director who used this software in her old organization. Unfortunately, she came from a much smaller locality.

What can you do?

Out To Pasture

SCENARIO #9

Meilin has been an excellent employee for over 27 years. She has always been interested in new things and has taken plenty of opportunities for professional development. Her new boss has come into the department with some wonderful new ideas and Meilin was excited about helping out.

For some reason her new boss thinks she is retiring soon, but she has no plans to do so. She has noticed every time she volunteers to learn one of the pieces of equipment she is told she has plenty to do and not to worry about it. Meilin is beginning to feel she is being put out to pasture.

What should Meilin do?

Sabotage

SCENARIO #10

Prior to the implementation of the new structure, Tom had been a good performer but was always a little negative and sarcastic about things he did not like. Since some of his job duties got changed, he has been intolerable often in public where not only his staff but customers may overhear him talking about how inefficient the organization is. You tried to ignore him for a while thinking he would get this off his chest and move on, but several months have elapsed and you see no progress. The worst part is he is passing on some of his negativity to a couple of new employees in the department he has been training.

What do you do with Tom?

ACTION PLAN

1. What am I going to tell my boss I learned here the past two days?

2. What am I going to share with my staff about the last two days?

3. What is one thing I can do differently right away?

4. What do I now know I am currently doing right when it comes to managing change?

Reading Resources

Abrashoff, Michael. It's Your Ship. Business Plus, New York, N.Y.; 2002.

Adams, Marilee. Change Your Questions, Change Your Life. Barertt-Koehler Publishers, San Francisco, California; 2004.

Bardwick, Judith. Danger in the Comfort Zone. New York: AMACOM, 1991.

Biech, Elaine. Thriving Trough Change. Alexandria: ASTD Press, 2007

Block, Peter. The Empowered Manager. San Francsco: Jossey-Bass, 1987.

Block, Peter. Stewardship. San Francisco: Berrett-Koehler, 1993l

Buckingham, Marcus. Go Put Your Strengths to Work. Simon and Schuster, New York, N.Y.; 2007.

Dalziel, Murray and S. Schoonouer. Changing Ways. New York: AMACOM, 1988.

Drucker, Peter. Innovation and Entrepreneurship. New York: Harper Business, 1993.

Feltman, Charles. The Thin Book of Trust. Bend: Thin Book Publishing, 2009.

Hammer, Michael and J. Champy. Reengineering the Corporation. New York: Harper and Row, 1985.

Hammond, Sue Annis. The Thin Book of Appreciative Inquiry. Thin Book Publishing, Bend, Oregon; 1996.

Hammond, Sue Annis and Andrea B. Mayfield. Naming the Elephants. Thin Book Publishing, Bend, Oregon; 2004.

Hiatt, Jeffrey M., ADKAR. Prosci Learning Center Publications, Lovelan, Colorado, 2006.

Imai, Masaaki. <u>Kaizen</u>. New York: McGraw-Hill, 1986.

Kanter, D. and P. Mirrus. <u>The Cynical American</u>. San Francisco: Jossey-Bass, 1989.

Kanter, Rosabeth Moss. The <u>Change Masters</u>. New York, Simon and Schuster, 1983.

Klein, Kim. <u>Fund Raising for Social Change</u>. Jossey-Bass, San Francisco, California; 2007

Kotter, John P., and Dan S. Cohen. <u>The Heart of Change</u>. Harvard Business School Press, Boston, Massachusetts; 2002.

Kotter, John P. <u>Leading Change</u>. Harvard Business School Press, Boston, Massachusetts; 1996.

Kouzes, James and Barry Z. Posner. <u>The Leadership Challenge</u>. San Francisco: Jossey-Bass, 1995.

Linden, Russell M.<u>Seamless Government</u>. San Francisco: Jossey Bass, 1988.

Morgan, Gareth. <u>Riding the Waves of Change</u>. San Francisco: Jossey-Bass. 1988.

Nadler, David, Marc Gerstein and Robert Shaw. <u>Organizational Architecture</u>. San Francisco: Jossey-Bass, 1992.

Naisbitt, John and Patricia Aburdene. <u>Reinventing the Corporation</u>. New York: Warner Books, 1985.

Osborne, David and Ted Gaebler. <u>Reinventing Government</u>. Reading: Addison Wesley, 1992.

Patterson, Kerry, Joseph Grenny, Ron McMillan, and Al Switzler. <u>Crucial Confrontations</u>. McGraw-Hill, New York, N.Y.; 2002.

Patterson, Kerry, Joseph Grenny, Ron McMillan, and Al Switzler. <u>Crucial Confrontations</u>. McGraw-Hill, New York, N.Y.; 2005.

Peters, Tom. <u>Thriving on Chaos</u>. New York: Harper-Collins, 1992.

Rath, Tom. <u>Vital Friends</u>. New York: Gallup Press, 2006.

Ryan, Kathleen and D. Oestreich. Driving Fear Out of the Workplace.
San Francisco: Jossey-Bass, 1991.

Thompson, Charles. What a Great Idea. New York: Harper-Collins,
1992.

Tichy, Noel and M.A. Devanna. The Transformational Manager. New
York: John   Wiley, 1987.

Leadership...Inspiring Oneself and Others

facilitated by

Carol Susan DeVaney, CPF, CPLP
DeVaney Wong International, LLC

OBJECTIVES

You will…

❖ explore the key elements that help us succeed in organizations.

❖ reflect with an appreciative eye on the leader you want to be.

❖ consider how to create a culture that helps you and others find passion and meaning in daily work.

Internal Mindset – Are you a problem solver or an appreciative learner?

Special Issues For Women – Flatness, blaming and long story.

KEYS TO SUCCESS

SKILLS	What special leadership skills do you bring to your organization?
UNDERSTANDING CULTURE	Do you know what cultural elements help people succeed in your organization?
360 SUPPORT	Who watches out and advocates for you above you, beside you and below you?
AGILITY	How quickly can you assess what you can contribute to charging realities?
INTERNAL MINDSET	Are you a problem solver or an appreciative learner?

Skills

1. Describe the things you do at work that make you feel energized and make the time fly.

   _____

   _____

   _____

   _____

   _____

2. List the top 4 things/people that are the most important to you.

   _____

   _____

   _____

   _____

3. What do you do at work that contributes to supporting those 4 priorities?

   _____

   _____

   _____

   _____

Culture

If you were mentoring a young woman who just moved into the industry what 3 or 4 elements of the business culture should you make sure she understands?

1.

2.

3.

4.

360 Support

1. How do you want to be described by people above you?

2. How do you want to be described by people beside you?

3. How to you want to be described by people below you?

What do you need to do to make sure that happens?

Agility

What specific examples could you describe that demonstrate your ability to shift and learn quickly?

The A B C Model

A Think of a situation that you think creates an obstacle for your leadership success. For example: I work full time yet also have to take care of my parents and my two children.

B Beliefs and Attitudes

C Describe how the situation makes you feel and how it affects you.

Draw a picture of yourself and symbols that represent the leadership role and the type of leader you want to be 5 years from now. What would your "provocative proposition" be?

Resources for Future Thought

Adams, Marilee. Change Your Questions, Change Your Life. San Francisco: Berrett-Koehler, 2004.

Bradberry, Travis and Jean Greaver. The Emotional Intelligence Quick Book. New York: Fireside, 2005.

Buckingham, Marcus. Go Put Your Strengths to Work. New York: Simon and Schuster, 2007.

Heim, Pat and Susan Murphy. In the Company of Women. New York: Penguin Putnam, 2001.

Rath, Tom. Vital Friends. New York: Gallup Press, 2006.

Succession Planning

facilitated by

Carol Susan DeVaney-Wong, CPF, CPLP
DeVaney-Wong International, LLC

OBJECTIVES

Participants will...

Develop a broader knowledge of
succession planning strategies

Be exposed to a strength based
model of employee development

Have the opportunity to have focused,
structured discussion on what
strategies might help the organization
achieve its goal of a strong pipeline
of talent for the future

Create next steps plan so the
discussion can lead to a road map
on how to address this critical human
capital issue

AGENDA

8:30 to   9:00 a.m.
  Welcome/Introduction/Group Agreements

9:00 to 10:00 a.m.
  What We Know So Far? Presentation from Group
  Participants

10:00 to 10:15 a.m.
  Break

10:15 to 11:45 a.m.
  Strength Video and Discussion

11:45 to 12:45 a.m.
  Lunch/Networking

12:45 to   1:30 a.m.
  The Gallop Strength Assessment as a Strength
  Based Model for Talent Management/Succession
  Planning/Employee Development

1:30 to   4:15 p.m.
    Ideas Into Practice-A Work Session
    (Break will occur about 2:15 p.m.)

4:15 to   4:30 p.m.
    Closing and Evaluation

Key Points to Consider

Instructions:

As your colleagues present the things that stood out for them in the reading materials, please jot down any concept you think the group may want to get back to.

NOTES:

Three Myths to Consider

	Myth	As you grow, your personality changes.
	Reality	As you grow, you become more of who you already are. What might be the implication of this for employee development?
1		

	Myth	You will grow the most in your areas of greatest weakness.
	Reality	You will grow most in your areas of greatest strengths. How might this impact your thoughts about IDP's?
2		

	Myth	A good team member does whatever it takes to help the team.
	Reality	A good team member deliberately volunteers his strength to the team most of the time. How might this affect how you think of helping develop your team's talent?
3		

I LOVED IT! 	**I LOATHED IT!** 
1	1
2	2
3	3
4	4
5	5
I LOVED IT! 	**I LOATHED IT!** 
1	1
2	2
3	3
4	4
5	5

What Helped You Succeed?

1. What key elements (skills, mentors, unexpected luck, growth of agency, etc.) helped you succeed at becoming a leader or potential leader?

2. How might this be the same or different for folks just starting in the organization?

3. How might this be the same or different for folks in the wings for increased opportunities for leadership?

4. If an old friend of yours had a brilliant daughter that just joined the organization which suggestion would you give her for being successful?

A Force Field Analysis

Instructions: As a small group, discuss the following questions and be prepared to discuss the following questions and prepared to do a short summary of your team responses.

1. What are the three main forces pushing for us to develop succession planning strategies?

2. What are the three main obstacles that are getting in the way of us doing this effectively?

3. What would be the risks of not doing anything?

4. What would be the risks of doing something?

5. If you had been invited to your child's career day at his college and we are successful at improving the succession planning strategies, what would you like to say to them 5 years from now about the organization and its opportunities for employees?

What Next?

1. What is one thing we need to stop doing as a result of our discussion today?

2. What is one thing I think we need to start doing as a result of our discussion today?

3. What is one thing I can personally do as a result of today's meeting?

How Did We Do?

On a scale of 1 to 7 with 1 being Poor and

7 being Excellent, how would you rate the following

statements?

_____	1. I feel we successfully completed the stated objectives.
_____	2. I believe the structure allowed for sufficient discussion considering we only had a day.
_____	3. I feel the facilitator kept us on track.
_____	4. I feel I am more informed about the directions we need to consider in Succession Planning.
_____	5. I feel like the group will be better able to tackle this issue in the future.

STRATEGIC PLANNING RETREAT

June 11, 2008

facilitated by

Carol Susan DeVaney, CPF, CPLP
DeVaney-Wong International, LLC

For your notes...

FLEXIBLE AGENDA

8:00 am – 8:30 am: Welcome and
Continental Breakfast

8:30 am – 9:00 am: Summary presentation
of Friday and Saturday's
Community Sessions

9:00 am – 10:00 am: Group Agreements and
Setting the Common Language for
Our Work

10:00 am – Noon: Personal and
Organizational Vision and
Provocative Proposition

NOON: LUNCH

12:45 pm – 3:00 pm: The Core Values, the
Mission, and the Strategic
Directions to Guide the Process

3:00 pm – 4:00 pm: Future Action and
Closing

Three Concepts Shaping U.S. Government At All Levels

Concept A – Entrepreneurial Government
Government Reinvention

Concept B – Seamless Government

Concept C – Government Alignment
Government Accountability

General Principles of Entrepreneurial Government

Don't just do – empower others to do
for themselves

Government is not about the existing
rules, it is about the mission and
desired results.

How much you do is not as important
as how much you achieve

You exist to meet the needs of your
citizens/customers not the needs of a
bureaucracy

Keep the focus on earning revenue,
not just on how to spend it

Get decision making to the most
efficient levels

Don't think about just more programs,
think about how the market and
policies can support the needed
direction

SEAMLESS GOVERNMENT

Government services should not be a
patchwork of poorly related services,
but an integrated system that appears
seamless to the consumer.

EASY POINT OF ENTRY

VERY LITTLE REDUNDANCY

GOVERNMENT ALIGNMENT

"The Government Performance and Results Act of 1993 seeks to shift the focus of government decision making and accountability away from a preoccupation with the activities that are undertaken – such as grants dispersed or inspections make – to a focus on the results of those activities, such as real gains in employability, safety, responsiveness, or program quality."

G.A.O.

MAJOR TYPES OF PLANNING

Strategic Plan
(3-5 years)

⬇

Tactical Plan
(1-2 years)

⬇

Project Plan
(Specific time project
will be completed)

⬇

Action Plan
Short term courses of action
to accomplish the strategic
plan
(2-3 months)

CREATING A VISION

VISION

A mental picture how
the organization will
LOOK, FEEL, and INTERACT
with its stakeholders
in the future.

What we can BECOME

VISION STATEMENTS

"Better things for better living through chemistry"
Dupont

"To provide memories"
Fuji Film

"The Heart of Silicon Valley."
Sunnyvale, California

"We want to be recognized as a dynamic organization that is able to efficiently provide the integrated service delivery needed to lead a rapidly evolving food and agriculture system."
United States Department of Agriculture

MISSION STATEMENT

A fairly brief description of what the organization would look like if the vision became a reality and the strategic plan was accomplished.

GREEN MOUNTAIN COFFEE

MISSION

"We create the ultimate coffee experience in every life we touch from tree to cup – transforming the way the world understands business."

SUNNYVALE, CA

MISSION

"A family-centered business, friendly, and always innovative city."

DANIA BEACH, FLORIDA

MISSION

Dania Beach
Historic Yet Undiscovered

"At the City of Dania Beach we are committed to providing responsive municipal services and improving the life for our citizens. This is accomplished through honesty and integrity, quality customer service, leadership with vision, restoring economic vitality, and embracing our historic heritage."

GUIDING VALUES

This is the organizations basic underlying or guiding principles that are the foundation for the vision.

USDA VALUES

Strong ethics

Service

Teamwork

Inclusive decision-making

STRATEGIC GOALS OR DIRECTIONS

Four to six guiding directions that will help the organization achieve its goals.

STATE OF FLORIDA
Strategic Directions

Keeping Florida's economy vibrant

Success for every student

Strengthening Florida's families

Keeping Floridians healthy

Protecting Florida's natural resources

Organization's Life Cycle

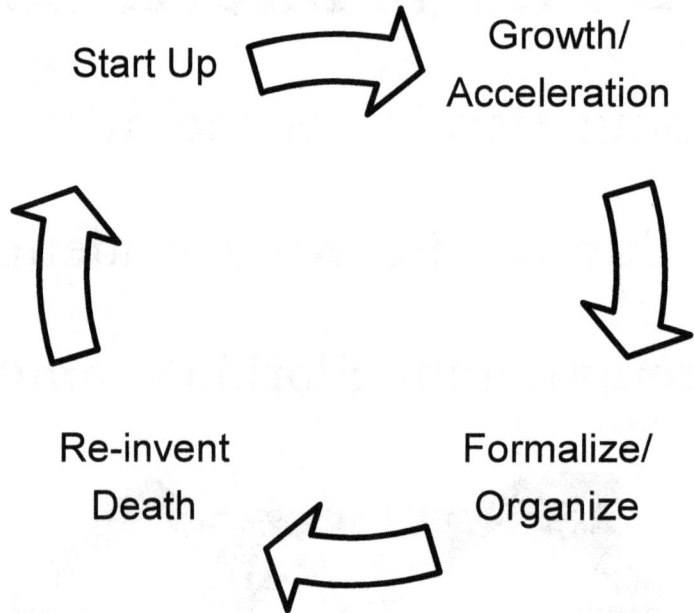

Start Up → Growth/Acceleration

Growth/Acceleration ↓

Formalize/Organize

Formalize/Organize ← Re-invent Death

Re-invent Death ↑

Nothing changes except for

PAIN

OR

GAIN

Appreciative Inquiry
and
The Provocative
Proposition

LINCOLN'S PROVOCATIVE PROPOSITION

"Four score and seven years ago our fathers brought forth on this continent, a new nation, conceived in liberty, and dedicated to the proposition that all men were created equal...that we are highly resolved that these dead shall not have died in vain – that this nation, under God, shall have a new birth of freedom – and that government of the people, by the people, for the people shall not perish from the earth."

GREEN MOUNTAIN COFFEE

Provocative Proposition

"We are motivated by a deep desire to learn, to share and to represent the best of corporate America – to be an organization working for a higher purpose, sustained by relationship as well as by profits. This is our journey, this is our quest."

Remembering Carol Susan

APPENDIX 1
Remembering Carol Susan

The Crone Speaks

Love at Work

I met Jim while working with a large government agency. He had been with them the whole 23 years since he got out of college. According to his boss and my HR contact he was being sent to my Change Management workshops because he was always in a rut, did not seem to have any enthusiasm and even with the exciting changes the organization was poised to make did not seem to have the least bit of enthusiasm for being part of the implementation team. This was a team of technical accounting folks who were getting ready to implement new software that could really change the way the agency does business.

The first morning of the class Jim seemed exactly as they had described-lethargic, disinterested and in truth somewhat dull. Then at the lunch break I saw him take a call and even though I could not hear what he was talking about he seemed very animated and happy. As he came back to class it was almost as if a burden had been lifted. He actually looked years younger. This intrigued me to no end so at the afternoon break I mentioned what I had observed. Jim shared that he is part owner of a rare books shop. He had been an English major in college and his dream had been to own a bookshop and write novels. He got married right out of college and felt he had to take a more sensible job to support his family. His parents urged him to get into government preferably in the money area as that was probably the last to get cut. The call that had come in was his business partner saying a rare collection Jim had been hunting down for a customer had been located.

The next day of the workshop at the break Jim brought in pictures of his shop to show me. He described how he just loves the smell and feel of books and the quirky clients who share his passion for literature. He told me the agency had provided a good living for his family and the people were nice enough but nobody he cared to spend time with. As he put it, he did what they asked him. It was almost as if he came alive when he left work.

I strikes me that we say to people work doesn't have to be fun. Ok, but maybe what we fail to say is that if you love the work you do and the people that do it with you what you have is a boundless source of energy to do it. Many of the folks that I have seen be successful in their work literally loved it. They loved the scents, the feel, the chatter, the product, the service-all of it.

We often focus all of our energy on promoting the golden handcuff in the name of retention. What if we freed those folks to pursue their dreams and brought in people who really care about what it is that we are about?

I know, I know, you are probably saying "Well, Carol Susan, there are some jobs that are just not lovable. Really? Perhaps the best example I had about this was a handsome young man whose job it was to stand guard at the local dump to keep folks from violating the dumping policies. He was probably the least educated and underpaid in a whole group of employee orientation participants. One of the questions we asked as an ice breaker was for people to tell us why they had chosen their new jobs. I figured he would say something like it is a tough economy and I needed a job. What he said instead took my breath away. He said, "I know I am not too educated but my Grandpa always told me it is our job to take care of our Earth. I have three children and keeping poisons out of our soil and water is what I can do for them and for your children. "The group was really quite for a few minutes and I could see the sudden appreciation for him from the other new employees. This is someone who loves their work and what it stands for. I heard many stories over the years about how Jake educated many long term violators at the dump always quietly and patiently explaining how what they wanted to do hurt them and their families. He never tired of being in the hot sun or the cold rain and always took his role seriously.

We are afraid to use the word love at work. However, is it not love that makes us work harder, better, and happier? Imagine if love was in your performance measures. Imagine asking "What would make you love what we do?" or "What would make you love the people you work with?" What I find is that in coaching clients around these questions it opens up what their hearts really desires and often they find that their jobs actually provides for that. Whoa-so am I saying you don't have to love your job? Not exactly, it is best if you love your job and the people you work with but it is also good if you can see the connection between your job and what you really love. Tom was a jeweler in a large landlocked city. Not a favorable job for a person who loves deep sea diving? Well, yes it was. Tom loved his job because the seasonal nature of it allowed him the freedom to go diving for extended periods in places he loved. He actually liked the beauty of the stones and the joyful moments he saw when people purchased special things for themselves and those they cared for, but what he really loved was the freedom his job provided.

Tom's boss is smart enough to know that Tom is one of his best sales people and most creative jewelers. He also knows that for that to happen he has to free him to pursue his deepest love which is diving. If Tom's boss did not have the desire to know what really makes his people tick he might have tried to provide monetary or recognition incentives which would be fairly meaningless in Tom's case.

LESSON # 1- Do you know what your employees really love? Or perhaps more important do you really care?

Painted Nails and Dark Stockings

When I was a young manager I always aspired to get an additional degree, another credential, another proof of my technical worth to the organization. Yet you know and I know that skill is not often the reason people get promoted or kept during a recession. My boss taught me a lesson I did not fully grasp at the time but the older I get the more I understand the wisdom of what he shared.

Mark was an open door kind of guy so when he called me into his office and closed the door immediately I wondered what terrible thing I had done. Perhaps my newest employees had violated a policy. Maybe I messed up in the budget projections I turned in two weeks ago? But no, Mark said, "Carol Susan, I have something to tell you and I do not know how you are going to take it." Now I was really nervous. He proceeded "We do not do dark stockings here." This was so out of the realm of what I thought our discussion was going to be that I think he assumed my silence was a signal to continue. "As a matter of fact, I noticed you paint your toe nails and that is not OK." I stammered "How do you know I paint my toe nails?" He responded "Well, you wore peep toe heels the other day and to be honest we do not believe in toe cleavage."

I guess Mark thought that had gone rather well as I did not have anything to say and simply walked back to my office. The truth was I was vacillating between thinking he was a pervert that had some foot fetish and trying to figure out what any of this had to do with my performance. My friend Denise is pretty level headed so I called her and ranted and raved about the incredibly dumb conversation I had just had. At one point Denise stopped me point blank and said "Is what he said true?" I became irritated accusing her of taking his side. She calmly said go look and call me when you have. I could not believe she wanted me to go look at what people were wearing on their feet. But by now my interest had peaked and I went around all three stories of the building. There were no dark stockings, no open shoes including the men who primarily wore tie type shoes, and certainly if anyone painted their toe nails you would never know it.

I began to think about what makes people successful in organizations and became more and more aware that skill was a small part of the equation.

Basically what I discovered was that four things help you succeed in an organization. One is skill which is sort of the basic. However, in most organizations there are plenty of people who are just as skilled as you are.

The second element seems to be how well you understand and can navigate the culture of the organization. Until Mark raised my awareness and understanding of the workplace culture I did not even know it existed. It reminded me of when I first came to this country my husband and I were walking in a mall and he got very irritated with me accusing me of walking on the wrong side. I had no idea what he was talking about. But once he explained it to me I saw the pattern. Every organization has a culture. Patterns and ways of behaving that people knowingly or unknowingly adapt to or stumble against. Without that knowledge it is very hard to succeed.

Third is what I call your 360 buffer zone. Successful people cultivate people below them, beside them and above them that open doors and provide both hazard warnings and a hand up to them. Often times we think we are too busy to get to hear the latest scuttlebutt or are fearful we will be seen as behind kissers. However, people at all levels around us have the ability to put in a good word for us at a critical moment or throw us under the bus on a whim. How many times have you seen an individual high performer's ability sabotaged because she did not take the time to build that important element of support?

Fourth is agility. In an era of specialization we crave agile people who can adjust to the newest market realities or customer expectations. People often fail because they find a skill set or a strategy that works today, but do not have the flexibility and agility to adapt to the changing needs of tomorrow or the next day.

LESSON # 2 Is your organization's carrot primarily build around technical skill? How do you help employees understand the other success factors in the job?

Dust Bunnies and Fresh Eyes

The longer I work the more convinced I get that the greater an expert we are at something the more difficulty we will have in determining how to solve serious problems in our area of expertise. Isn't it funny how much break through innovation has come from people looking at things with fresh eyes. As a consultant I know I am not smarter than most of my clients, my secret weapon is a fresh look.

Let me tell you what I mean. Being a small business I like to support small business when I can. There is a little ethnic restaurant not far from me who has a delicious buffet at lunch. The cost has to be kept with certain parameters as folks tend to have a limit on what they are willing to spend for lunch. Betty told me one day that they were loosing money on the buffet and that if this did not improve it would be impossible to stay open with just their dinner crowd. She went on to say the thing that made her sad was she wanted people to eat their fill and enjoy it but that she could make a profit if they just did not leave a bunch of expensive food on their plates.

I looked at the buffet and at the left over plates and noticed the leftovers were the more expensive ingredients in the buffet such as chicken breast, meat, and fish. There was very little left over rice, beans, vegetables or salad. It occurred to me that the buffet was set up with the most expensive ingredients at the front of the line and the cheapest at the end. Diners would fill their empty plates with the expensive stuff and have very little space for the cheaper dishes. I suggested she try putting the salads first followed by rice and vegetables and then the more expensive dishes. What she discovered was that people would fill their empty plates with the less expensive dishes and then they would put the meats on The result was less waste of the meats and an amazing rise in profits with no complaints from the diners.

So why did Betty not think of this herself? I call this the dust bunny problem. Have you noticed that when guests come to your home the dust bunnies reproduce like crazy? Now you know that you are a tidy person, but these dust bunnies just want to embarrass you in front of company. The fact is we live in our homes and get very complacent about what is around us it is only when we have guests and have the opportunity to see things with fresh eyes that we notice things that have been there for quite a while. How many of us are looking and looking for an object just to have someone point out that it is right in front of us?

This is why vacations, sabbaticals, going away to training or retreats, shadowing, hiring new talent, sharing people resources, and yes, consulting work. These are all ways to help us look at what we do with fresh eyes.

LESSON #3 Make sure you always are expecting company. See things with fresh eyes.

Carol Susan DeVaney-Wong
June 26, 2009

Fighting Back

Good evening. My name is Carol Susan DeVaney and I am struggling with pancreatic cancer. As you probably know, pancreatic cancer is the least survivable cancer and over 95% of us diagnosed will die from the disease within two years. We do not know what causes it and we do not know how to prevent it. I am here only because of the skill of the dedicated people at Johns Hopkins and the determination of my daughter not to let me accept defeat.

I am honored to be asked by Cynthia and Stanley Bloom to share a few minutes with you tonight and would like to dedicate my message to my friend John Brown who died of lung cancer a couple of weeks ago, and to the Blooms' beautiful daughter Vail who taught cancer a thing or two.

As I go to chemo appointments and meet my brothers and sisters, gray skinned and often hairless cancer warriors, I am consistently amazed by the strength of the human spirit. Cancer can rob us of many things. Some are big things – in my case it robbed me of my ability to make a living, it took my husband's job, it will mean giving up our home, any opportunity for a comfortable retirement, and the ability to casually promise my daughter that in the future I will dance at her wedding and be a good grandma. It also robs us of small things-my ability to eat many of my favorite foods, sleeping soundly through the night, traveling without a virtual pharmacy of medications, and buying large bottles of shampoo without wondering if I will be around to finish the whole bottle.

Being angry is ok. It beats the heck out of being depressed which immobilizes us from action. Before being a cancer survivor I was a cancer care giver. I remember when my Mom had breast cancer and my Father and Step-father had lung cancer how angry I was that they had to suffer so and how frustrated I was that no matter what I did I never felt I could offer enough care, enough support to make it all better. Being angry raises our energy level momentarily but ultimately at the end it leaves us exhausted. I can truly say my parents' graciousness as they fought their battle set the tone for my own battle and for that I am most thankful. I learned that anger gets us off the couch, but for the real battle we need other weapons.

While on this journey I have discovered a few armaments that have helped me fight back. The first thing is to name and embrace the enemy. When I was first diagnosed my husband and my friends could not say the word cancer. Many

385

wanted to minimize the horrific diagnosis with well meaning platitudes. I found it important to identify it and claim it. Without doing this it is like shadow boxing. Once you name it others feel comfortable talking about it and it creates the opportunity for a clear vision of what you need and how others can help. It is no longer the boogie man that we have to talk about in whispers, but the challenge that others can play a role in helping you overcome. It is ok to say "Yes, I know most folks don't make it through this, but this is what I hope happens to me- I dream of being around to be an old lady, and if that is not possible I hope to enjoy many more days of joy, laughter and love." What I found is that others will rise up to the challenge as a formidable army of true believers, and try to make your dream come true.

Indulge me for a moment. For just a minute close your eyes. Now think of a memory when someone did something loving for you. Remember how you felt at that moment. Now keeping your eyes closed think of a time when you made a loving gesture towards someone else. Remember how that felt. Now open your eyes and look at the faces of those around you. What expressions do you see? In my experience when people think of loving moments there is great satisfaction and feelings of well being.

I was warned by many not to share my diagnosis. People would be uncomfortable, they would distance themselves, and I might find myself alone. I threw all caution to the wind and told my family, friends, and work colleagues the truth and asked for their support. The expressions of love I have received have created a veritable wall protecting me from the daily challenges of living with cancer and lifting me up in my darkest moments. I had prayers and mediations said for me in churches, synagogues, mosques, Reiki circles, and energy groups all around the world. It is all good. There was some interesting research that was done asking groups to pray or send positive energy to patients in ICU. The patients who unknowingly were the recipients of this love fared better than the control group. I truly believe the loving energy and the loving gestures that have surrounded me have been my biggest ally in this fight. I have witnessed and benefitted from the strength of those close to me like my amazing daughter, Taryne, and the love of my life, my husband Eldon, but I have also experienced the generosity of spirit from unexpected sources. Outside of our homes we are afraid to use the word love because we are concerned it will be mistaken for sexual love. My diagnosis took a lot from me, but when I risked opening up my soul to others sharing my fears and dreams in exchange I received the greatest gift of all knowing in my life time- not at my eulogy -how much I am loved. All the money in the world will not give you that kind of satisfaction. Cancer gave me the gift of unlimited love. The love has come in various forms-a kind word, a funny gift, a plate of food, a joint moment of tearfulness or laughter, or just standing by. I have had family members, friends, former students, employees, old bosses, clients, neighbors, and folks who I came into frequent contact with while I shopped look me straight in the eye or send me open hearted letters telling what I mean to them. Some folks will say, "Yes, Carol Susan, but all the love in the world won't save some of us." Ok, agreed. It may not save me. But would you want to miss out on this experience? Not me-I'm going for it. It may not cure me but it will keep me whole as long as I am here.

And finally I have discovered what I call my high definition life. Like the new TVs I have experienced life in a most vivid way. I think of what I want to remember about that very moment in case I do not experience it again. I try not to waste energy on things that at the end do not matter and have exquisite focus on the things that really do matter. The question becomes –if I really do have limited time-and by the way we all have limited time-is this the way I want to spend it? It is a freedom that only comes once we understand the truth of our finiteness. Another gift from cancer.

So naming the enemy, welcoming love, and remembering what really matters can give us if not a fighting chance a memorable and meaningful end to our journey. Join me in a standing ovation for the all the cancer warriors past and present, their heroic care givers, and their army of loving supporters. Every single one of you makes a contribution to a life well lived. Thank you.

Carol Susan DeVaney-Wong
Relay for Life
Coral Springs, Florida
April 30, 2010

A Sample of Customers Includes...

American International Group
AES Consulting Engineers
American Household
American Institute for Banking
American Safety Razor
ABB
Association of Planning Directors
Banta Publishing
Broward County
Centex
Chubb
Clemson University
CMAA
Commonwealth of Virginia
Crestar Bank
Dade County Federal Credit Union
Environmental Protection Agency
Federal Reserve Bank
Fire Chiefs Association
George Washington Hospital Center
Gold Coast Builders
Henrico County
Hewlett-Packard
The Government of Hungary
Hospital Corporation of America
International Association of
Firefighters (AFL-CIO)
International Personnel
Managers Association
Kentucky Credit Union League
KPMG Peat Marwick
Landmark Design Group
Latin America Personnel Association
Lee County
Local Government Attorneys
J. E. Jacobs

Microsoft
Michie Publishing(Lexis-Nexis)
Milgo Solutions
Montgomery County
Nestlé
NOAA
Nortel Networks
Owens and Minor
Panamá Chamber of Commerce
Prince William County
Quaker Oats
Racal Security (Zaxus)
Sensormatic(Tyco)
Seventeenth Judicial District Judges
Sibley International
Signet Bank
Smith-Kline Beecham
Stafford County
Sunbeam
University of Maryland
University of Richmond
University of Virginia
Virginia Commonwealth University
Florida Atlantic University
VML Insurance
U.S. Army
U.S. Department of Agriculture
U. S. Department of Education
U.S. Department of Commerce
U.S. Department of Transportation
U.S. Navy
Urban League
Well Point
The World Bank

and many other

Carol Susan DeVaney, CPF, CPLP

With over 30 years of experience using a strength-based approach to helping individuals and organizations manage change, Carol Susan has a proven track record in the field of organizational learning and performance. She has provided organizational development, small and large group facilitation, executive coaching, troubleshooting, and training in both fluent English and Spanish throughout the U.S. and abroad including customers from countries like Argentina, Jamaica, Mexico, Costa Rica, Hungary, China, and Panama.

She has been President of DeVaney-Wong International, LLC since 1989 serving a variety of groups in government, nonprofit, family owned and Fortune 100 companies. Sample clients include ABB, AIG, American Safety Razor, Banta, Centex, Chubb, Jacobs Engineering, HP, Landmark Design, Michie Publishing, Microsoft, Nestle, Nortel, Smith Kline Beecham., Quaker Oats, Owens and Minor, Racal, Sensormatic, Sibley International, Sunbeam, Well Point/Anthem , Gilda's Club, Zaxus, University of Virginia, University of Maryland, Florida Atlantic University, Montgomery County, City of Warrenton, Henrico County, NOAA, USDA, USDOT, EPA, the US Army and Navy and many more. She is a United Nations preferred provider.

Carol Susan has her undergraduate and graduate degrees from Catholic University in Washington, D.C., receiving her Masters the week of her 21st birthday with honors. Her undergraduate had a special interest in world philosophy and religion and her graduate degree is in Social Work. She has published and or has been featured in articles about Organizational Development, Change Management, Multicultural Issues, and Stress Management in publications such as *Vision Humana* (a Latin American HR Journal), the *Journal of Medical Economics, O.D. News, and HR Magazine*. She is currently focused on the impact of the Positive Psychology movement and the use of Appreciative Inquiry.

Active in her professional organization, ASTD, she has received one of its highest honors, the International Torch Award. In addition to presenting frequently at ASTD events, she has also received an

Excellence in Practice Citation for her work in Global Diversity, and a Volunteer-Staff Partnership Award. She served on three local boards and three national committees including being the Chair of the 12,000 participant International Conference in 2002 which brought professionals from almost 100 countries. Carol Susan helped establish ASTD's first Global Network overseas. She teaches ASTD's Certificate Program for Facilitating Organizational Change. She has appeared in the Marquis *Who's Who in America and Who's Who in the World*. Carol Susan is a Certified Professional in Learning and Performance, a Certified Professional Facilitator with the International Association of Facilitators, a Professional Futurist Member of the World Future Society, she has been active in SHRM as Florida's Diversity Director on the Council for HR Florida, and a member of South Florida OD Net. She also maintains an active License in Clinical Social Work in the Commonwealth of Virginia.

Born and raised in the Republic of Panama to multicultural, multilingual parents, Carol Susan has special expertise and a personal interest in the impact of global economics and culture in today's workplace, which stems from her early work as a health educator and community organizer with high-risk populations, plus specialized training in Women Issues and Prevention and Health Promotion. She is the coauthor of *Workforce Diversity* which she wrote in 1989 and has been an HRD Press bestseller for almost 20 years, used in organizations of all types and sizes. She also was a contributing author in *Prevention in Community Mental Health.*

Carol Susan DeVaney, CPF, CPLP

Carol Susan DeVaney has been President of DeVaney-Wong International, LLC since 1989. She focuses on helping individual and organizations successfully manage change in an increasingly challenging and diverse environment. Fluent in both English and Spanish she has provided organizational development , small and large group facilitation, executive coaching , troubleshooting and training for teams in many countries including the US, Argentina, Mexico, Costa Rica, Hungary, China, and Panama.

Carol Susan has worked effectively with all levels of organizations including the C-Suite. A sample include ABB, AIG, American Safety Razor, Banta, American Household Centex, Chubb, Jacobs Engineering, HP, Landmark Design, Michie Publishing, Microsoft, Nestle, Nortel, Smith Kline Beecham, Quaker Oats, Owens and Minor, Racal, Sensormatic, Sibley International, Well Point/Anthem , Gilda's Club, Zaxus, University of Virginia, University of Maryland, Florida Atlantic University, Montgomery County, City of Warrenton, Henrico County, NOAA, USDA, USDOT, EPA, the US Army and Navy and many more.

Carol Susan has her undergraduate and graduate degrees from Catholic University in Washington, D.C., receiving her Masters the week of her 21st birthday with honors. Her undergraduate had a special interest in world philosophy and religion and her graduate degree is in Social Work with training in both community organization and clinical practice. She is a Certified Professional Facilitator and a Certified Professional in Learning and Performance. She maintains an active clinical license in the Commonwealth of Virginia.

Samples of her work in the area of D & I and Global Competencies include:

- Helping create a leadership team with global competencies for a merger of EU and US companies.
- Executive coaching for country managers as they assumed leadership roles in different countries.
- Recovery troubleshooting after public concerns about discriminatory practices or insensitive behavior in organizations.

- Helping governmental and private organizations do a diversity audit and integrate D & I into their strategic directions.
- D & I and global competencies training.

She is the primary author of *Workforce Diversity* and a contributing author in the textbook *Prevention* and in the *Workforce Diversity Field Guide Supplement*. She has published in, or has been featured in articles about Organizational Development, Change Management, Multicultural Issues, and Stress Management in publications such as *Vision Humana* (a Latin American HR Journal), the *Journal of Medical Economics, O.D. News, and HR Magazine*. She is currently focused on the impact of the Positive Psychology movement and the use of Appreciative Inquiry.

Active in her professional organization, ASTD, she has received one of its highest honors, the International Torch Award. In addition to presenting frequently at ASTD events, she has also received an Excellence in Practice Citation for her work in Global Diversity, and a Volunteer-Staff Partnership Award. She served on three local boards and three national committees including being the Chair of the 12,000 participant International Conference in 2002 which brought professionals from almost 100 countries. Carol Susan helped establish ASTD's first Global Network overseas. She teaches ASTD's Certificate Program for Facilitating Organizational Change. She has appeared in the Marquis *Who's Who in America and Who's Who in the World*. Carol Susan is a Certified Professional in Learning and Performance, a Certified Professional Facilitator with the International Association of Facilitators, a Professional Futurist Member of the World Future Society; she has been active in SHRM as Florida's Diversity Director on the Council for HR Florida, and a member of South Florida OD Net.

Born and raised in the Republic of Panama to multicultural, multilingual parents, Carol Susan has special expertise and a personal interest in the impact of global economics and culture in today's workplace, which stems from her early work as a health educator and community organizer with high-risk populations, plus specialized training in Women Issues and Prevention and Health Promotion

DeVaney-Wong International, LLC

Carol-Susan DeVaney, CPF, CPLP

WORK HISTORY

November 1990   **President/Owner, DeVaney-Wong International, LLC**
to Present(P/T1989)   Hollywood, Florida

Full-time, independent, bi-lingual organizational consulting and training in the U.S. and abroad. Provide organizational consulting in areas such as Strategic Planning, Capacity Building, Change Management, and growth and performance issues. Facilitate live and virtual groups for team building, inter-team dialogue, problem solving, redesign issues, and community dialogue.

Extensive experience in executive coaching focused on specific performance issues or for general development. Have developed leadership programs for lead workers to senior executives.

Have provided specialized training in Facilitating Organizational Change, Customer Service, Diversity, Communication, Building Community Dialogue, Leadership Development, Ethics and other topics. Clients have included Federal, state and local government, private, closely held, family run, academic and non-profit organizations.

Responsible for supervision of subcontractors, budgeting, procurement, contracting, and all other aspects of running the business. Have a wide working relationship with Universities, OD and training consultants and suppliers, and professional associations.

A sample of clients include the US Army, USDA, USDOT, EPA,SmithKline Beecham, Quaker Oats, Chubb, American Safety Razor, Nortel, Nestle, USDA, Sunbeam, Commonwealth of Virginia, Montgomery County, Broward County, Henrico County, Gilda's Club, Landmark Design, Centex Homes, Jacobs Engineering, Wellpoint, HP, and many more. She has won joint awards with her clients including in Customer Service and Diversity.

Carol Susan is a Certified Professional Facilitator, a Certified Professional in Workplace Learning and Performance, a professional futurist with the World Future Society, and an LCSW in Virginia. Currently SHRM's Diversity Director for the 28 State of Florida Chapters.

December 1986   **Administrator, Organization Development and Training**
to November 1990   County of Henrico

Managed the Division of O.D., Training and Special Services. Responsible for planning, organizing, delivering, contracting and evaluating training for 27 departments with an employee complement over 3,000. Organizational development, consultation, coaching and counseling to top management, division heads and supervisors. Facilitated strategic planning, problem solving, and team-building meetings. Designed and implemented a Management Development program that resulted in national awards for Management Development, Strategic Planning, and Volunteer Services. Designed a Customer Service Program using TQM models, which also has received national recognition and an award. Integrated a Managing Diversity process into all HRD and HRM services.

Consulted to the EEO Committee and Employee Assistance, and assisted in recruitment, promotion and other personnel functions as needed. Responsible for the County's Rules and Regulations, Tuition Reimbursement, Volunteer Services (1,300 volunteers) and Basic Skills (Reading, Writing and Math) Training Programs. Supervised professional and contractual employees. Responsible for budget, procurement and annual reports.

January 1981   **Coordinator of Business Program**, Prevention Department
to November 1986   Chesterfield County, Chesterfield, Virginia

Full-time trainer and consultant to business, industry, governmental agencies, schools, physicians, churches, and civic and community groups. Developed and delivered training in: Supervision and Management Development, Listening, Conflict Resolution, Stress, Time Management, Effective Meetings, Communication, Problem Employees, Male/Female Communication, Cross Cultural Differences, Family and Work Life Issues, and others. Consulted on organizational issues such as Decreasing Resistance to Change, Effective Policies and Procedures, Clarifying Company Values and Objectives, Outplacement, and others. Excellent skills in needs assessment, planning, and implementation of training programs. Provided extensive individual coaching to numerous supervisors and managers, plus served as a resource in EAP-related issues. Facilitated internal and external meetings including community meeting between agencies and key leaders. A good example was the growth of the County's Committee on Aging. Established Critical Incident (PTSD) Program for Public Safety Personnel. Helped organize a citizens' group in a high-crime, low-income housing unit, addressing the issues of women and minorities. Also provided support to a multinational on cross-cultural issues of locating in Chesterfield County. Facilitated the development of a program to respond to critical training manual on Stress Management, brochures, fliers, newsletters, press releases, and other written communication. Appeared on numerous TV shows, newspaper features, radio shows, and did frequent public speaking to groups such as the Rotary Club, Lions, Jaycees, and others. Developed and hosted a monthly cable TV show. Supervised professional staff, students, and volunteers as needed. Consulted and provided training to the County's "Wealth of Health" Committee. Small clinical caseload.

June 1979   **Clinical Social Worker III**, Outpatient Department
to January 1981   Chesterfield Mental Health Center, Chesterfield, Virginia

Supervised professional staff and master's level interns. Consulted with human service agencies, health organizations, schools, and community groups. Provided traditional counseling services to individuals, couples, families and groups. Special Stress Management and Divorce Adjustment groups. Special interest in mental health and women. Selected by NIMH to participate in a 25-member national study group on Women and Mental Health. Special consulting support to WIC and other Social Services programs. Public speaking and adult educational groups on a variety of topics.

January 1977   **Psychiatric Social Worker**
to June 1979   Brevard County Mental Health Center, Cocoa, Florida

Provided traditional counseling services to individuals, couples, families and groups. Consultation and training to HRS agencies, employee assistance programs, schools, group homes, and private physicians and clinics. Specialized counseling to recent Spanish-speaking immigrants and older clients. Public speaking on a wide range of topics including communications, conflict resolution, EAP programs, and stress management. Facilitated meetings between varied agencies including United Way agencies, half way houses and community based addiction programs.

March 1976 to January 1977	**Coordinator of Social Services** Brevard County Mental Health Center, Cocoa, Florida

Coordinated with a head nurse and MD in the delivery of services for a 12-bed alcohol detox unit. Provided supervision for professional, support staff, and students. Training and consultation provided to employee assistance programs (EAP), local Air Force Base, police, half-way house, colleges, and civic organizations. Facilitated planning and problem meetings for community agencies as needed. Individual and group counseling and community organization..

April 1975 to March 1976 Maryland	**Community Educator** Prince George Health Department, Adult Services, Cheverly,

Developed a patient education manual, brochures, and other training materials. Provided Stress Management training. Coordinated training and consultation efforts with the American Heart Association, American Pharmaceutical Association, Regional Medical Planners, and others. Developed and delivered a mass media educational campaign which included newspaper stories, radio spots, talk shows, TV shorts, health fairs, and public speaking in both English and Spanish. Responsible for specialized programming for high-risk Black, Asian and Hispanic communities. This was in response to the negative perception of community health programs after the Tuskegee Syphilis Experiments became public. Supervised grant staff. Facilitated community meetings between community leaders and organizations trying to serve them. Individual and family counseling regarding stress management and lifestyle adjustment issues. Grass roots community organizing as needed.

June 1974 to March 1979	**Addictions Counselor** Prince George Bureau of Addictions, College Park, Maryland

Summer and part-time evening work involving alcohol and drug counseling. Supervised two bachelor level staff members. Taught alcohol educational groups. Consulted with local colleges, DWI programs, employee assistance programs, and others. Public speaking to community groups. Established one of the first programs nationally to use multiple-family therapy with substance abusers.

PROFESSIONAL MEMBERSHIPS

American Society for Training and Development (National, Ft. Lauderdale and Miami)
ASTD International Torch Award
ASTD International Conference Chair
ASTD National Advisor for Chapters
ASTD Excellence in Practice Citation
ASTD Volunteer Staff Partnership Award
V.P. Program Development, Ft. Lauderdale

V.P. for Programs, Washington D.C. Chapter
National HRD Career Committee
President, Greater Richmond Chapter
Founded National ASTD's Ibero-Americano Group
Helped found ASTD Panamá Global Network
NASW, ACSW, and LCSW (Virginia)
International Facilitator Association
Professional Member of The World Future Society
Society for Human Resource Management (National, Ft. Lauderdale and Miami)
SHRM's Director of Diversity for the State of Florida/HRFlorida
Europe's *Brind Register* of Customer-Recommended Consultants, 1993-2000
  (*Register* closed)
Marquis' Original *Who's Who in America and Who's Who in the World (multiple years)*

EDUCATION

Bachelor of Arts. Received in May 1974 from Catholic University of American in Washington D.C. Member of Pi Gamma Mu and Sigma Epsilon Phi Honor Societies. Graduated Cum Laude. Completed 4 years in 3 years. Minor in world religion and philosophy.

Master of Social Work. Received in May 1975 from Catholic University of America in Washington D.C. Special accelerated student, completed two years of graduate work in one, with honors.. Mix of clinical, community organization and group work. MSW the week of my 21st birthday.

Continuing Education. Extensive continuing education including MBTI Trainer certification, Effective Instruction, Strategic Planning, Media Image, and others. Selected by NIMH for a 30-member national group to study issues related to mental health and women. I maintain my Clinical License in the Commonwealth of Virginia. Attend as well as present at ASTD and SHRM conferences.

CPLP/Certified Professional in Learning and Performance and CPF/ Certified Professional Facilitator.

SPECIAL SKILLS

Born and raised in the Republic of Panamá to multi-racial, multi-cultural parents. Speak, read, and write fluent English and Spanish. Special interest in culture, class, religion, gender, and other differences and their impact on the workplace teams and performance..

ADDITIONAL EXPERIENCE

2001 to present   **Adjunct Faculty for Special Projects**
                         Florida Atlantic University Institute for Government

1981 to 1983   **Instructor**, Women's Resource Center and Management Institute
> University of Richmond, Richmond, Virginia
> Part-time instructor.   Taught course titled "The Life of the Corporate Wife."
> Presented several "brown bag" topics around family and work issues. Presented a
> workshop to spouses of MBA candidates.

1977 to 1979   **Instructor**, Rollins College
> Patrick Air Force Base, Florida
> Taught a variety of courses attended mainly by military personnel and local
> businessmen, including Interviewing, Human Sexuality, the Psychology of Aging,
> Divorce, Group Dynamics, Counseling, Human Behavior, and others.

1974 to 1975   **Internships**
> Nine months each at the Laurel Maryland Mental Health Center and at the
> National Children's Medical Center in Washington D.C. Advocacy and counseling
> with a wide range of clients. Volunteered as a Roving Leader in a street front
> advocacy agency working with Hispanic and African American street gangs in the
> Columbia Road area of DC. Coordinated outreach services with community faith
> groups.

PUBLICATIONS

> Featured in numerous professional publications such as *HR Magazine, OD News*
> and *Journal of Medical Economics*. Authored a chapter in a textbook called
> *Prevention in Community Practice* published by Brookline Press and *Managing
> Diversity*, a book, manual, and video published by ITC and distributed through
> HRD Press as their best selling diversity product since 1993.

DeVaney-Wong

Workbook

CD Availability

and

Other Books

APPENDIX 2: Other Information

DeVaney-Wong Workbook
CD

Purchase Information:

To purchase the *DeVaney-Wong Workbook CD* go to www.devaneywong.org to place your order. The cost of the *DeVaney-Wong Workbook CD* is $15.00 which includes priority shipping by USPS. Secure e-payment is provided by Stripe. The *DeVaney-Wong Workbook CD* will be mailed upon receipt of your payment.

Questions/Contact Information:

Please email C. Eldon Taylor, Publisher at celdontaylor@gmail.com with questions. I will respond as quickly as possible.

DeVaney-Wong Workbook CD contents for handouts (Word documents – 372 pages) and powerpoint presentations (357 slides) follow.

DeVaney-Wong Workbook CD Contents

Word Documents

COMMUNICATION and CHANGE (132 pages)
Effective Communication & Conflict Management (32 pages)
Managing Change: Practical Knowledge and Skills
    In Today's Changing Workplace (30 pages)
Managing Change Pre/Post Tests (2 pages)
Understanding Your Role in Change: Being an Effective
    Change Agent in Your Organization's Culture (64 pages)
Change Management: Competency Elements
    and Behaviors (3 pages)
Change Songs: Remember These? (1 page)

DIVERSITY & INCLUSION (112 pages)
Diversity & Inclusion As A Change Initiative (16 pages)
Mastering Diversity and Inclusion (36 pages)
Developing Cultural Competencies for Work in Global
    Environments (6 pages)
Mining The Gold: A Diversity Initiative (4 pages)
A Brief Introduction to Crossing Cultures (10 pages)
The Art of Global & Cross Cultural Competencies (14 pages)
Diversity in Latin America (18 pages)
How to be a Diversity Chair (8 pages)

LEADERSHIP (128 pages)
Effective Communication & Crucial Discussions
    for Leadership (32 pages)
Strategically Leading Change (50 pages)
Leadership...Inspiring Oneself and Others (10 pages)
Succession Planning (10 pages)
Strategic Planning Retreat (26 pages)

372 pages total

Power Point Documents

COMMUNICATION and CHANGE (104 slides)
Effective Communication & Conflict Management (35 slides)
Managing Change: Practical Knowledge and Skills
      In Today's Changing Workplace (20 slides)
Understanding Your Role in Change: Being an Effective
      Change Agent in Your Organization's Culture (48 slides)
Change Management: Competency Elements
      and Behaviors (1 slide)

DIVERSITY & INCLUSION (129 slides)
Diversity & Inclusion As A Change Initiative (15 slides)
Mastering Diversity and Inclusion (37 slides)
Practical Tips for Creating Inclusion (15 slides)
Developing Cultural Competencies for Work in Global
      Environments (5 slides)
Mining The Gold: A Diversity Initiative (2 slides)
A Brief Introduction to Crossing Cultures (11 slides)
The Art of Global & Cross Cultural Competencies (15 slides)
Diversity in Latin America (18 slides)
How to be a Diversity Chair (11 slides)

LEADERSHIP (124 slides)
Effective Communication & Crucial Discussions
      for Leadership (31 slides)
Strategically Leading Change (50 slides)
Leadership...Inspiring Oneself and Others (11 slides)
Succession Planning (12 slides)
Strategic Planning Retreat (25 slides)

357 ppt slides total

Other
Books

Hellfires of Grief: Love Poems

C. Eldon Taylor

A collection of 222 poems written after the disembodiment of my beloved Carol Susan. I use the word disembodiment rather than the word death or death to the body since my beloved's beautiful radiant spirit left her physical body to return to our spirit realm home. The words in my journals were inadequate to express my experience of loss, grief, and despair. I converted the raw words of grief in my journals into poems to express in words the language of my tears, broken heart, and the hellfires of grief. Hellfires of Grief summarizes the day time experience of the first eighteen months of bereavement.

Available from Amazon: (362 pages) 6X9 soft cover
      Soft cover: $16.00 ($14.22 Prime)
      Kindle: $7.00

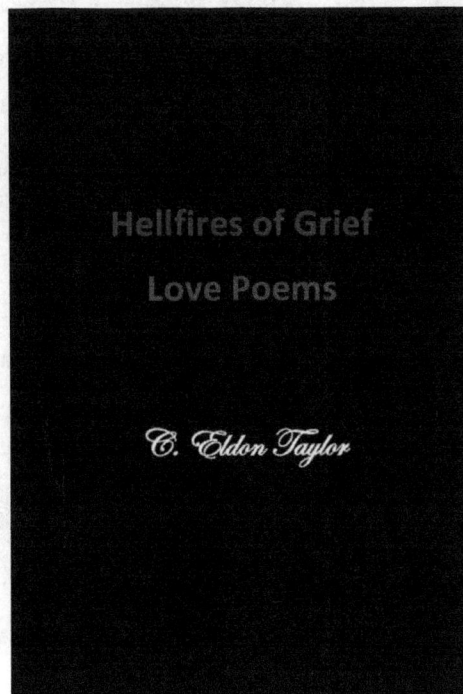

Golden Dreams
Companion to Hellfires of Grief: Love Poems

Carlos Eldon Taylor and **Carol Susan DeVaney-Wong**

A collection of 111 poems describing the golden dreams shared by Carol Susan and Carlos Eldon after the disembodiment of Carol Susan. Carol Susan reaches from beyond to share her golden healing energy. Carlos Eldon travels to the spirit realm to visit with his beloved in shared golden dreams. Golden Dreams is the counter point to Hellfires of Grief providing Carlos Eldon with the wonderful golden love of his celestial soulmatespiritmate.

Available from Amazon: (200 pages) 6X9 soft cover
    Soft cover: $13.00 ($11.12 Prime)
    Kindle: $6.00

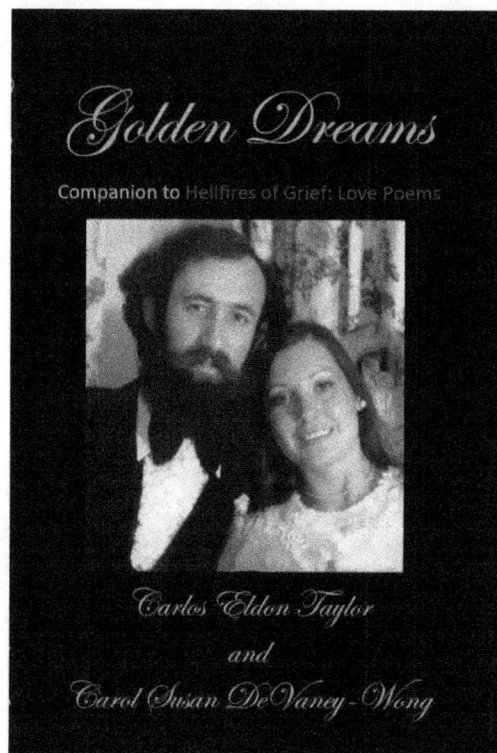

Hellfires of Grief II: More Love Poems

C. Eldon Taylor

A second collection of 222 poems written during the second eighteen months of bereavement. Hellfires of Grief II: More Love Poems summarizes the day time experience of the second eighteen months of bereavement.

Available:

On or before October 31, 2014

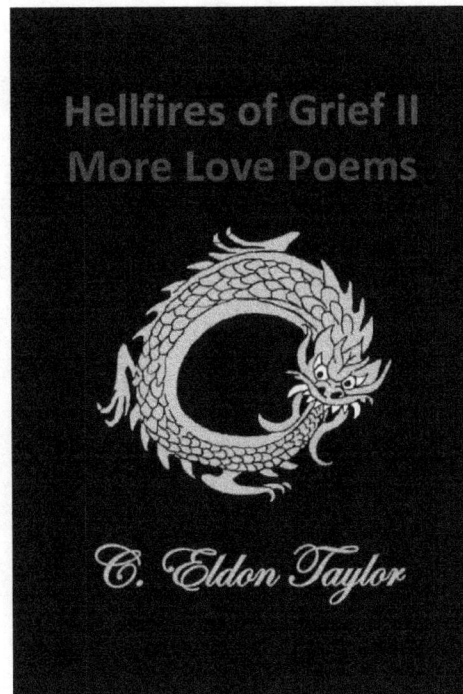

Golden Dreams II

Companion to Hellfires of Grief II: More Love Poems

Carlos Eldon Taylor and Carol Susan DeVaney-Wong

A second collection of 111 poems describing the golden dreams shared by Carol Susan and Carlos Eldon after the disembodiment of Carol Susan. Golden Dreams summarizes the dreamtime experience of the second eighteen months of bereavement.

Available:

On or before October 31, 2014

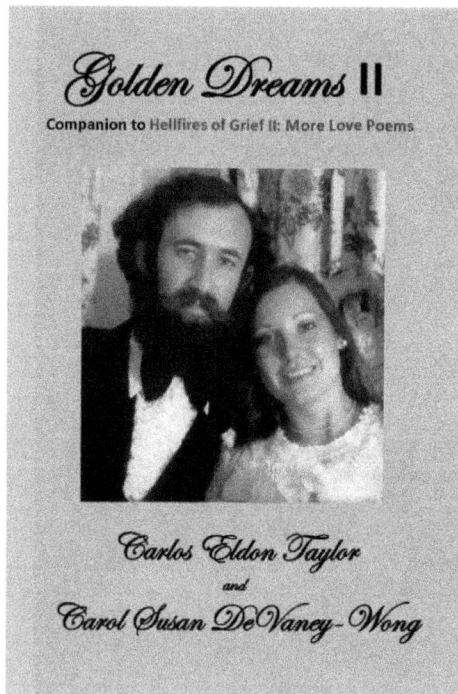